POSITIVITY

@

THE WORK PLACE

RE-THINKING WHAT'S RELEVANT
FOR BETTER WORK PLACE DESIGN

VISTASP BHAGWAGAR

PARTRIDGE

To order additional copies of this book, contact
Partridge India
000 800 919 0634 (Call Free)
+91 000 80091 90634 (Outside India)
orders.india@partridgepublishing.com

www.partridgepublishing.com/india

```
        ┌─────┐ ┌─────┐
        │ A.  │ │ B.  │
        └─────┘ └─────┘
┌─────┐ ┌─────┐ ┌─────┐ ┌─────┐
│ C.  │ │ D.  │ │ E.  │ │ F.  │
└─────┘ └─────┘ └─────┘ └─────┘
┌─────┐ ┌─────┐ ┌─────┐ ┌─────┐
│ G.  │ │ H.  │ │ I.  │ │ J.  │
└─────┘ └─────┘ └─────┘ └─────┘
        ┌─────┐ ┌─────┐
        │ K.  │ │ L.  │
        └─────┘ └─────┘
```

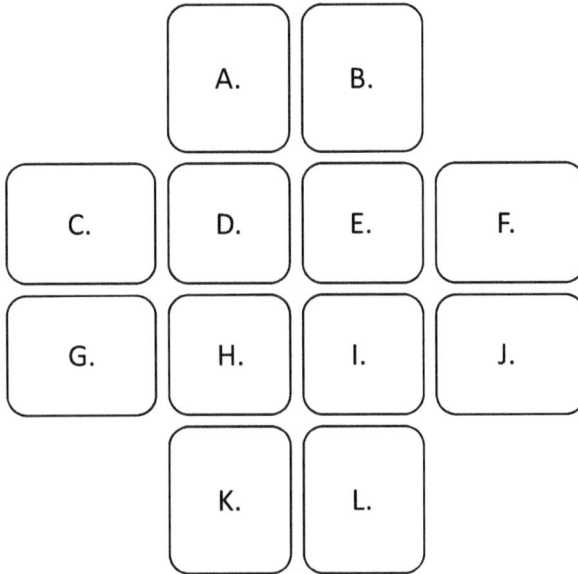

The Interpretation of the Cover:

The Cover Denotes the PLUS for Positivity @ The Work Place thru Combination of very many factors covered in this books such as, but not limited to:

A: Resimercial Design (Homing from Work)
B: The Hybrid Model (Working From Home)
C: The Office as the "Collaborative Club"
D: Inverting Maslow's Hierarchy of Needs (@ Work Place)
E: The Human Centric World
F: The SOCIAL Aspect of the Workspace: WE
G: Flexibility & Agility @ The Workspace
H: The Multiplicity of Seating Options
I: The Private Work Zone: The ME Zone
J: The Stepped Arena for Group ideation
K: The Group Huddle, Training & Brain-storming
L: Biophilic Design: The Outside Inside

Cover Design: AVA Design Pvt Ltd, India

CONTENTS

Chapter 6
Basic Needs 2: Better Work Space "Process Design".......... 185

Chapter 7

Good Design is NOT Google Searching!
Good Design is about Soul-Searching!
And then Designing "A La carte"!

Vistaspeak

The Foreword

Author Vistasp has such a rich experience to share with his vast 30 years of Experience in Work Space Architecture -Thank you Vistasp!

The knowledge, The Learnings, The Journey, The Evolution of Design at Workplace!

Today, it is a Fortune to get the insights HOW we all should look at the Future of the Workplace!

Who better than Vistasp!

Pandemic / New Mindset - How do we want to leverage the workspace?

Positivity @ Workplace -amazing thinking to bring this on top of the elements we should all work with, at the conception stage of space planning.

Maslow's theory of Motivation! the way we create design space to enhance and add Motivational quotient!

Happiness/Culture will drive us all to Re-Think the design and Build from here.

I recommend all to Learn from this amazing collection of insight and experience sharing!

Wishing you the very best.

Best wishes

Pinny Mann

Senior Portfolio Manager India, Microsoft India

(She is a Corporate real Estate leader empowering people and organisations with customer obsession outlook)

The Preface

In a year when the Word "Positive" has mostly had negative connotations, this book is all about bringing Positivity into the work place, where we typically spend the most meaningful waking hours of our lives!

Having spent 30 years in the line of Work Space Design, this book is an attempt to demystify and decode the RIGHT DESIGN Approaches to bringing Positivity in the Work space; something that my team and I have been conscientiously doing for decades! Multiple awards, seminars, juries and post Covid Webinars later, my friends have convinced me that this knowledge needs to be passed on to those who seek to build on a long journey in Work Space design! I started from Zero with no guru or mentor in this field.

I hate the word "Offices" and have gone to great lengths to ensure its minimal usage across the Book. Offices denote a Medieval Mindset, akin to factories of the Industrial age, and should no longer be used in Work space parlance, particularly Post Pandemic. The Office signifies a formal place, which it no longer is meant to be; the "Workspace", in contrast, could be anywhere: home, office or somewhere in between!

Work Space design has evolved over the last thirty years: in how we conceive of it, in how we design it, in how we expect the end users to use it. This is because much has changed in what work is all about today; how it is done and where it needs to be done! The Book revisits Maslow's famous Hierarchy of Needs as a basis for understanding Human needs at the work place and interestingly advocates an inverted look at this profound theory in contemporary times.

While, as a Work Space Architect, I do not claim to be a Work Space Psychologist or a Human resources Expert or a Peoples Excellence Strategist: I can claim to have worked with the best of these categories, over the last 30 years! All my clients and colleagues have been my teachers. The Book presents an "Architects'" understanding & Point of View of what works and certainly what "could work" if applied in parts, to creating better positivity @ the work place.

As Architects / Work Space Designers, our tribe are trained to conjure up space-based solutions that can promote positivity in mental and physical health at the workplace. However, they fail to deliver, if the design ideations are implemented in a stand-alone manner, that does not align with a holistic and comprehensive approach to wellness & wellbeing at the work place. This book looks at creating positivity @ the work space by using design as a holistic device to advance physical, operational, and social aspects of human health, productivity, and wellbeing.

This Book is also about passing the Baton of Knowledge forward to the New Generation of Architects, Designers and all those interested in what, why and how Positivity in Work spaces can benefit its end users. The Book addresses all the concepts thus far that are relevant to my mind, as well as approaches that make sense to do justice to Work space design. The book is written in a Simple Structured manner and can be browsed across any chapter, though it benefits a start to finish read for the first-time reader! Use this Book as a Play book (a Friend, Philosopher & Guide) that allows you to prioritise what one must do and often, what one must not... to make our Work Spaces Positive!

Enjoy it and write back to me on <u>arvistasp@icloud.com</u>

Vistasp Bhagwagar

March 2021

The Introduction

"We shape our buildings; thereafter they shape us," said Sir Winston Churchill in his speech to the meeting in the House of Lords, October 28, 1943. How true, even today.

Almost three Fourths of a century later, we can say the same applies to our Work spaces! The Way we conceive them, shape them, and inhabit them affects the levels of engagement and productivity of a Work Space! After all, Given the amount of time we spend at work, it's worth working out what needs to be done to make the work space experience positive.

This book does not refer to work spaces as "offices". The very connotation of an "Office" denotes exclusivity: The "Corner office" or "The Cabin" are often discriminatory and suggest only the "Part", Not the "Whole"!

Work space Designing is about being inclusive, Equitable and consistent: from the receptionist to the corner cabin and the highest echelons of the organisation! It needs to tie up all the parts like beads on a necklace.

This Cord of connectivity between the diverse parts makes for a good work space! The Cord may often

be a vision translated in different ways for different organisations! The Cord is like a Thread of Ideas that may work for one and not for the other! But it needs to be there...

Why is this Book So relevant today?

Because it takes a renewed Post Covid view of Maslow's Hierarchy of Needs in contemporary Post Covid Times and repositions the way we look at the theory!

Because it insists that the Physical Work space, post covid, is as important if not more important than any other human need, at the work place.

Because, with people wanting to get back to collaborate & socialise at work, we need to understand what makes these spaces positive and how relevant is the work-space today.

Because the Future of the Work-space, as an ideology, needs to be re-looked at with new lenses and with a new purpose, if it's to exist, or remain relevant!

This book makes some promises: it's a first that ensures you enter the mind of an architect and understand the complexities that he deals with in terms of how Work spaces need to be designed! It also hand holds you to the many layers of thought and vision that need to over lay to make an idea fructify and bear fruit! Undoubtedly, the most important aspect of this book is to break down the many concepts that are relevant to designing meaningful work spaces so that the end user also can make a better and more informed choice.

It talks of the "Process of Design" and also the "Design of the Process" to achieve Greater Positivity at the Work Place!

In that sense, this book is all about the end user and how to make a Work place more Positive, Engaging and hence Productive! It is not just for Architects, Designers but also for Clients, HR and FM Leaders and Visionaries who shape the offices where others work! It is also for the guy sitting quietly in the corner seat of any office who yearns for a better office and presents this book to his boss as they plan a new office for the future!

But whatever the case, the book makes a strong case for Architects to be central to the "design" process and "process" design for the new Post Covid Work place!

Chapter 1

Problems @ The Work Place

"Leaders, think and talk about Solutions.

Followers, think and talk about the problems."

Brian Tracy, Internationally Acclaimed Author of 21 books on Self Improvement

Introduction to Chapter 1

Let's look at the Developed World!

The Harvard Business Review talks about there being too much work place stress and cut throat competition, that not just harms productivity, but is also counterproductive to engagement, wellness and well-being.

Even in the pre pandemic era, as per research (Seppala & Cameron, 2015) whilst many people believe that stress and competition, at work, pushes towards better, faster and improved performance, there is a major price to pay:

1. *First, health care expenditures at high-pressure organizations are nearly 50% greater than at other similar places. The American Psychological Association estimates that more than $500 billion is siphoned off from the U.S. economy because of **workplace stress**, and 550 million workdays are lost each year as well thru stress at work. 60% to 80% of workplace accidents are attributed to stress, and it's estimated that more than 80% of doctor visits are due to stress. Workplace stress has been linked to health problems ranging from metabolic syndrome to cardiovascular disease and mortality.*
2. *Second is the **cost of disengagement**. While a cut-throat environment and a culture of fear can ensure engagement (and sometimes even excitement) for some time, research suggests that the inevitable stress it creates will likely lead to disengagement over the long term. Engagement in work — which is associated with feeling valued, secure, supported, and respected — is generally negatively associated with a high-stress, cut-throat culture. And disengagement is costly. In studies by the Queens School of Business and by the Gallup Organization, disengaged workers had 37% higher absenteeism, 49%*

more accidents, and 60% more errors and defects. In organizations with low employee engagement scores, they experienced 18% lower productivity, 16% lower profitability, 37% lower job growth, and 65% lower share price over time. Importantly, businesses with highly engaged employees enjoyed 100% more job applications.

3. ***Lack of loyalty*** *is a third cost. Research shows that workplace stress leads to an increase of almost 50% in voluntary turnover. People go on the job market, decline promotions, or resign. And the turnover costs associated with recruiting, training, lowered productivity, lost expertise, and so forth, are significant. The Center for American Progress estimates that replacing a single employee costs approximately 20% of that employee's salary.*

This section builds on what are the work place problems and what are the present-day stresses that cause these issues. First the Story...

1.1 The Story of 9-2-5: The Work Zombie

This is the story of Mr Nine to Five: we call him "the 925 Work Zombie" who lived in an office that was on the outskirts of a big city. It was the kind of place that was in an old dilapidated industrial area with high ceilings and small Windows

that looked out nowhere. It seems they were involved in Publishing books and journals!

It really did not matter, and in many ways, was perfect for the zombie, as it allowed him to move around the place without being seen. The zombie blew the candles to his fifth year in business at this place! The office was also five years old and the owners did not even realise this achievement. This did not bother the zombie so long as he managed to find his prey!

Five years ago, with much fanfare the office was inaugurated and the first prey for the Work zombie was Adrian, a strapping young man who had joined the office for not all the right reasons! He had only wanted to ensure he earned a salary and made ends meet. Perfect for the first catch! No one saw when the zombie bit him! Adrian did not bother too much about the kind of work he was doing so long as he got his monthly payments and worked exactly from 9 to 5 pm. He came on time, interacted with few, did his work and left for home on time. Introverted and self-contained. Adrian is still around and is the most silent worker in the office and lives a zombie life, in many ways himself.

Binny was a young lady who joined soon as the company secretary in the very first few months and worked long hours with great diligence. She was the blue-eyed girl of the boss as she did all she was told. She only did what she was told. She was the next Zombie prey! She got bitten by the Zombie in the very first week. She still works hard and does not worry about anything else beyond what's she needs to know.

Chan was the noisiest of the lot! He came in, as a happy go lucky soul who loved to laugh and crack jokes. But slowly realised that there were not many like him around and settled for a desk in the corner! He was the zombies next victim and the most prized prey, as happy people were difficult to snare! Great joy for the zombie! Chan works with head phones on and talks to himself often in the washroom!

The office also grew with more people coming into the same space that was designed for far lesser. Seating became tighter and the make shift cafe was removed and replaced with wall facing work stations! The company found the cafe unproductive and a wasted real estate. The joke was the washrooms and meeting rooms would be next! The business grew and the joke came true! Books started piling up on the floors and between desks creating walls between people!

And so, five years passed with dozens of zombie victims coming and going! The zombie grew stronger and lived a happy life thriving on innocent victims that fell prey to his moves. In fact, he loved the place as he did not have to go out to look for his victims! They seemed to come and stand in line to get bitten!

The work zombie lives in all of us ...and bites us, even without us knowing!

Adrian lacked ambition to grow beyond just serving the hours he had been contracted for. There was no attachment to work or work place! Without the attachment how could there be any connect with a positive mindset!?

Binny was very diligent and very hard working and ready to do all that she was told. But there was no initiative and no sense of camaraderie with others! Without social interaction and bonding, the work place was just a place to work! Nothing more.

Chan was a story of a person changing from an extroverted mindset to one who stayed within himself as his workspace did not offer him too much scope for collaboration and social exchanges!

The office in the story lacked the desire to evolve and grow into a positive work space that cared for its employees rather than the top and bottom lines! The priorities were "to get work done", not "how best to get it done" and certainly not "what it wanted to achieve " as a shared goal with all its stake holders!

These are the sort of offices where the 925 Work Zombie thrives! Offices that lack the spirit of camaraderie, bonding, interpersonal conversations, group sessions and collaborations suffer from being bitten by the Work Zombie! The 9 to 5 work attitude sets in at the cost of initiative, leadership, accountability and sense of ownership! There was no Work Culture!

Moral of the story: work places need to energise and get the best out of its occupants thru very active means and strategies. Thru Work Culture and enablement thru well designed physical spaces! Good design leads to good business! It's the starting point of creating employee engagement with a workspace!

The story does not end here. But the story of the work zombies ended two years later when the company was acquired by a large international publishing house!

The new management made several changes, first and foremost being relocating to a city centre that was easier to reach and closer to a bustling nerve centre of the city. Next, they recruited a work space architect who advised them to do things the right way and select a new office location that had wonderful large windows with light, views and ventilation.

The zombie hated the architect!

He did everything that made the zombie worry: he made the new work place with more social areas, central conversation / story reading arena and defined enclosed areas for storage. Formal Meetings rooms were complimented with high counter break out areas and coffee dispensing stations. Cabins were replaced with more open cubicles and work stations without barriers. Flexible seating and multipurpose spaces meant more could be done with the same space! A lighter and colourful workspace was created with write able walls where users could write and express! Large video walls echoed the company's new visions and goals and achievements! Birthdays were celebrated and events were made the most of in town Halls! Engaging conclaves and booth seating and good lighting ensured a new vibe to the work place!

The cafe was merged with the reception into a work lounge like a new age hospitality lobby. It had vibrant graphics, fresh plants and soft background music! The work place became autonomous, agile and activity based. Washrooms and rest spaces were made with panache. Everyone was happier, more engaged and business grew, twice over, in half the time!

The zombie died, as there were no takers for negativity! He cursed the architect and simply vanished from the minds of all who he had bitten!

And Adrian, Binny and Chan lived happily ever after and completed twenty years each in the same organisation! They managed to vaccinate themselves against the 925 Workspace zombie!

Living proof of Good Design being Good Business! Workplace Positivity is all about infusing passion thru designed strategies and work space designs that work to create magic! Let's discover the science behind this!

What Ails many work spaces? What makes some places tick more than others? How do we define the ideal work spaces? Perhaps it's best to first review and dissect what are the many problems new age work spaces deal with day in and day out and how to alleviate them thereafter!

According to the International Psychology Clinic, (The 10 Most Common Problems People Have at Work and How to Solve Them, n.d.) the ten most common problems at work place has more to do with things that managers and administrators need to deal with rather than architects; it's well worth knowing these:

1. Lack of Training
2. No Two-Way Communication
3. Lack of Job-Related Accountability
4. Lack of Facilities
5. Ineffective Employee Recognition
6. Inadequate Job Descriptions
7. Excessive or Improper Company Policies
8. Dealing with Change
9. Difficult Clients or Patrons
10. No Way Forward

Whilst these can be dealt with better hands-on intervention from concerned HR Managers and Policies, the fact remains that they are fodder for the 925 Work Zombie who is ready to cash into any of these and take over your mind!

1.2 The Lack of Purpose

What a year 2020 has been!

The year 2020 has all made us realise that Work Spaces are Passe. Or so we think. Or so we are made to think. Actually, nothing is further from the truth! A river always flows and charts a new course, even if it is damned (pun intended)! Similarly, Work spaces / offices are here to stay even as we find new reasons against it or new forms for it! It will change course, but it will stay! It is as important to the urban landscape as a river is to the natural habitat!

The Office is HERE to STAY! It would evolve and would change as we go along and open up our work places back to the returning masses, post the pandemic. But yes, it needs to evolve and iterate into something more meaningful for all of us.

The One learning from the Pandemic is that we can work from anywhere! We always knew that and often worked from the car or the Coffee shop or the vacation, in some exotic destination in the past. But the pandemic taught us that work can be done equally well from home, or so we think.

What we have really learnt in this Pandemic is NOT whether we want to go to office or not whether we can work from home or not! What the Pandemic has given all of us is time to Pause, reflect and introspect! We have really learnt to understand what is the true Purpose of ourselves and our Work spaces!

How many of us actually get indoctrinated in an office in the right way? Do we get to be introduced to the larger picture of what we are doing as a group, how we go about our work and why we do so? Often, we are ONLY told that "This is the way we do things here, but never WHY this is the way we do things"?

If the Core of the existence is not explained, how can there be attachment? And if Attachment is missing, then how can there be engagement; without engagement, there can be no productivity; without which there can be no sense of contribution and Positivity!

There needs to be a purpose to every existence and for this... an existence of a purpose is equally important! Good Work spaces treat employees as humans and not as machines. Therein lies the most complex part of a work space! While every other organisation (factory, production house, Construction site etc) can be slowly replaced by AI and the like: the work place remains Unique as it needs the most complex of all creatures in existence: Humans!

HR would never be a key department in most offices, but for the need to control this species. The need to ensure that human beings perform requires the need to ensure they are in a positive frame of mind! That's why HR rules strongly in any and every Work space.

The key for every work space, thus, begins in the head; it begins in the very ideation of what the organisation is all about and how much can it indoctrinate others into that vision and mission! It is here that the seeds are sown for Positivity and productivity!

Thus the "WHY" is the pre-dominant question to be answered in the Work place even before it is physically built! The "WHAT & HOW" to be Built follows and would be answered in subsequent chapters...! Once importance is given to this, all answers follow.

As Mark Twain famously said: The Two Most Important Days in your life are the day you are born and the day you find out WHY?

1.3 FOMO (Fear of Missing Out)

A new term "FOMO" (Fear of Missing Out" has taken the Millennial Mind by a storm! We want to be everywhere. We want to be where the action is, we want to be where the buzz is and where things seem to move!

What Is FOMO? The fear of missing out **refers to the feeling or perception that others are having more fun, living better lives, or experiencing better things than you are. It involves a deep sense of envy and affects self-esteem. It is often exacerbated by social media sites like Instagram and Facebook. The Millennial Mindset needs to feel connected and wired to all that is happening and when it misses out on this, it creates a sense of deprivation and misery and negativity! Everything extraneous is an event or an occurrence that is needed to be connected to.**

There is a constant sense of comparison in this type of a mindset between what I have and what you have! **FOMO** manifests itself in various ways, from a brief pang of envy through to a real sense of self-doubt or inadequacy.

FOMO is of course nothing new, since as humans we are designed to feel a bit insecure or disappointed if we think we've missed an opportunity that others have made the most of. So why has this concept recently struck a chord with us, and so much so that we've suddenly invented a new expression to describe it? Predictably, the answer is connected with new technology, and social media in particular. Platforms such as Facebook, LinkedIn, Instagram and Twitter make it instantly obvious to us what other people are 'up to'. If we are not there, we are...not "there"!

This is where a Work place contributes! By having a work place that connects and contributes to a sense of happening and learning and interacting, the work place gets a new meaning!

People seem attracted to places that make them feel Positive: these are spaces that have the BUZZ of life and are "happening". Often this can have a lot to do with Location of the work place! If its in a busy Metropolitan hub with social spaces around, FOMO is less; However, for out of central city locations, the need for the office to fill the void becomes more important.

The fact is that people tend to think that there is great need to be in the centre of things; so if the office is not in the centre of things, there is a sense of missing out on life!

FOMO can be countered by suitably infusing the work place with the right design elements that stimulate an activity-based work approach and sense of learning and interaction, that will be covered in forthcoming sections. It makes a lot of sense for new offices to understand the new millennial mindset and either locate in happening hubs or make the office a social hub itself!

Often work spaces need to be energised thru better WIFI to enable work on the GO and to be able to catch up on the gossip! That's the single reason why Coffee shops like Barista, Starbucks and Café Coffee day see so much of transient office crowd working from there.

People like to be seen and like to see! There is a sense of happening and being "part of the crowd" that has been robbed away from us, by the Pandemic. This cup of desire is waiting to be fulfilled in the new age office! Nothing beats the feeling of being acknowledged and being part of the gang and dressing up to be with your friends at work! Good offices must see themselves as Social spaces that make this happen!

There is also a growing belief that FOMO needs to be countered with the idea of SLOW LIVING, which is to reject consumerism and embrace a more holistic life approach! More on this later, but suffice to know that Positivity at work place is intrinsically linked to the Mindset of the worker there!

1.4 The Factory Like office

Offices have been in existence since the Industrial revolution and have undergone several changes from the times of the "factory office: where people were compartmentalised into silos and almost considered non-human.

The factory office had other priorities; it was only about results and about maximising outputs! The Human element was missing and the factories operated in shifts to maximise profits and returns.

Cut to offices of the day and the case is entirely different! Human resources are the MOST Valuable and indeed the highest percentage of expense goes towards this heading followed by real estate & maintenance in any office! Typically, 10% is the cost of CRE while 90% is the Cost of people according to most experts in the work field domain!

There is thus, a greater understanding that the Factory Offices of today are more human resource based and need servicing of the human mind more than ever before! This has brought in the need for large Human resource departments, events and appraisals that are all tuned to make the human being perform at more optimal levels of performance! The happier the human mind, the more is the sense of productivity!

And so, we need to design our work places in manners that promote the New Age feel of being in a Happy Space, not in an erstwhile factory. The mindset change has been there in Employees & business owners who now feel the need for engaging work spaces that make employees want to come to work.

There are studies being done in different parts of the world on "How Happy you are to go to office"! Called the Happiness Index, this varies in different parts of the world. While in the US and Canada this would be 33%, it is very low at about 6% in India! The Global Average is about 15% and that indicates there is a lot of catching up to be done in this area!

One of the authors of the report John Helliwell in a statement said, "The happiest countries are those 'where people feel a sense of belonging', where they trust and enjoy each other and their shared institutions. There is also more resilience, because shared trust reduces the burden of hardships, and thereby lessens the inequality of well-being."

While these facts may represent cities and states at large, they are also indicators of how people living in them feel! The office can be seen as a microcosm of the real-world facts! It is the world of work for us! It is the part of the world we spend the most productive hours of our lives, day in and day out!

The need for Happiness at Work is the need for Greater productivity through better engagement!

Laura Putnam best describes an engaged employee as "one who works with consistency and passion. collaborates well with others, spread positive energy throughout the organisation and contributes great ideas. Companies with an engaged workforce do much better, almost five-fold! Having engaged, high performance employees can catalyse a chain-reaction: better service, increased customer satisfaction, higher sales, increased profits and ultimately higher returns for the share-holders!". (Putnam, 2015)

Putnam goes on to state that "as per Gallup, 70% of workers in the US are disengaged ... leading to building toxic environments, bringing other co-workers into a negative spiral and driving away customers !" (Putnam, 2015)

That's exactly what the 925 Work Zombie story was all about: Disengaged Employees! Factory offices are a thing of the past and new Age offices are the antithesis to them. Positivity and "Feel Good Factors" come in from the need to enable office to become ENABLERS that allow for chats, conversations, co-creation and the like.

Offices of the past are no more spaces we go to work in. Pandemic or no pandemic, there is need to redefine and evolve to a more human and interactive version of an office if we are to see Positivity at work place in reality!

In the book "Make More Money by Making Your Employees Happy," Dr. Noelle Nelson explains how employee happiness is directly correlated to the company's approach. What she has found is that when employees feel their company cares about their interests and makes them feel appreciated, then employees are more invested in the interests of the company. (Cooper, 2012)

1.5 The People Recipe Problem

Richard Branson, CEO of the Virgin Group comprising of 200 companies in more than 30 countries should know a thing or two about people! He has famously said "When it comes to Business Success, it's all about people, people, people!"

The **"People Recipe"** is perhaps the most important aspect of an office; it's the ingredients of the recipe for success at work; you need all sorts of people to make the office and this mix is ever important to consider when designing for them.

Two is company, Three is a crowd, may have connotations for out of office relationships, the fact is that when you put more than four people in a room, it becomes a crowd! And here we are dealing with offices, where scores of people work together every day!

Studies show that People personalities can be classified in Four ways:

1. **Energy Levels:**

    Extroverts: Who love working with other people on teams and busy places
    Introverts: Who like working independently in small groups and in calm quiet places

2. **Thinking Styles:**

Sensors: Who like working with concrete things like people, machines and data Intuitives: Who like working on abstract things like theories, ideas and possibilities

3. **Life Styles:**

Judgers: who like organisation and a structured, orderly workplace
Perceivers: Who like Flexibility and Freedom and don't mind a bit of chaos.

4. **Values Style:**

Thinkers: who want work that uses their intelligence and lets them excel.
Feelers: Who want work that reflects their values & helps other people

Now imagine having offices with a random mix of such personality types! It would be one thing to design for a given mix; but then offices are always in transient state with people coming in and going out! Offices need to be resilient to deal with this and when they are not, that's where the problem lies!

Good offices allow for the right mix of user types and allow for the freedom for all sorts of personalities and work types.

The sad reality though is that offices seem to be designed for Stereotypes: in some cases, they are not even gender friendly.

There are offices that are often not even Special needs adaptable. Most offices do not even abide by sanitary requirements for different genders, leave alone transgenders. Most do not even have adequate facilities for all: wash room counts being far less than specified.

The Sad reality is also that the offices are designed in a manner that do not take into account disparities in People Types: All people are assumed to be extroverted, though typically 66% people are introverts as per experts in this field! Offices consider all People to be having similar work styles and similar work profiles! Most Work spaces imagine everyone has similar levels of education and exposure, which is good! But what is not good is that Most offices feel that same work space typologies work for all! The Truth is they don't.

Most offices are designed less for humans and more for Humanoids! They are designed for No feelings. Places without feelings do not evoke attachment or association and are less engaging and so much lesser productive! Simon Sinek has rightly said: When People are Financially Invested, they want a return; when they are emotionally invested, they want to contribute!"

1.6 Burnout (Pre-Covid)

Let's get back to the developed world, where Burnout had been a bigger worry than the pandemic in a pre-pandemic time. Statistics show that people's jobs can contribute to workaholism, insomnia, and divorce. (PREMACK, 2018)

- The average American spends 90,000 hours at work over their lifetime.
- But 87% of Americans have no passion for their jobs.
- And 80% of US workers are outright dissatisfied with their jobs.
- One University of North Carolina study showed that half of marriages in the US with a workaholic spouse end in divorce — compared to 16% of marriages without one.
- A third of managers in the UK say they're losing their sense of humour because of work.
- And nearly 60% say their jobs are making them insomniacs.
- And a quarter of Americans say work is their No. 1 source of stress.
- In the US, stress from work is estimated to be the fifth-biggest cause of death.
- In Japan, hundreds of Japanese workers die every year from "karoshi," or death by overwork. That might involve suicide or simply dropping dead at their desks.
- 40% of millennials say they "feel guilty" for using all of their vacation days.
- And the majority of Americans don't even use all of their vacation days; there were 705 million unused days off last year nationwide.

Not everybody loves going to work. The 925 Zombie, in us, wakes up every now and then and weighs us down. Often, we get afflicted with the Burn Out Syndrome when we find ourselves drained of energy, exhausted and de-motivated.

Burn Out is often mixed up with routine work stress. It's very different. Stress is what shows on your face; Burn out is when you do not show up at all!

More than just increased stress, burnout causes overwhelming exhaustion (Physical & Mental), feelings of cynicism and detachment from your job & Colleagues, and a sense of ineffectiveness and lack of accomplishment, at work.

There are three types of work place Burnouts as per Dr Maslach (MacKay, 2020) :

- **Individual burnout** is caused by excessive negative self-talk, neurosis, and perfectionism. In other words, when you place extremely high standards on yourself or believe nothing you do is good enough.
- **Interpersonal burnout** is caused by difficult relationships with others at work or at home. For example, an aggressive or unwelcoming boss or co-worker can compound the stress you already feel at work to the point of burnout.
- **Organizational burnout** is caused by poor organization, extreme demands, and unrealistic deadlines that make

you feel like you're missing the mark and that your job is in danger.

"Highly stressful workplaces are often poorly designed, socially toxic, and exploitative environments. Why should such workplaces be given a free pass, when they are the sources of stress, while their inhabitants are being told that burnout is their own personal problem and responsibility?" as per the paper (MacKay, 2020).

Burnout can be fought by allocating proper time for work and rest; by focussing on progress and not just the end goal; by setting up priorities and not trying to do all; by Structuring your day with must do and could do tasks AND by reducing unnecessary stress makers in your life: whether its people, places or events.

Well said by Designer Frank Chimero: "Fatigue happens to your body, but burnout exhausts your soul."

To offset these stresses most organizations have allowed for a variety of perks ranging from Coffee shops, to Gyms, Creches, nap rooms, meditation rooms etc. Despite this, Not Surprisingly: A Gallup poll showed that the work space users prefer workplace wellbeing to material benefits. Wellbeing comes from one place, and one place only — a positive culture. (Seppala & Cameron, 2015)

More on this later!

1.7 Covid and its Impact

Mindboggling facts are revealed on the true impact of Covid on our work lives!

Whilst we all thought that COVID was a Blessing in disguise and indeed some of us have called it a "Good Virus" that allowed us to rekindle a work life balance, the reality is that the work day has on average increased by 20%.

The facts are very scaring, as they emerge from a report, (COVID-19:, 2020) wherein 1200 US workers were analysed in 2019 and then 2020; following were the four key findings:

a. **U.S. workers were stressed before COVID-19**: now, stress levels are through the roof Before the onset of COVID-19, nearly 60 percent of workers shared that stress had brought them to tears at work, a 23% increase from 2019.
Surveyed following the onset of COVID-19, workers report that their stress levels are significantly higher:

- 88% of workers reported experiencing moderate to extreme stress over the past 4-6 weeks.
- 69% of workers claimed this was the most stressful time of their entire professional career, including major events like the September 11 terror attacks, the 2008 Great Recession and others. Every demographic, including adults over the age of 55, rated COVID-19 as the most stressful time.
- 91% of employees working from home reported experiencing moderate to extreme stress.
- 43% of employees have become physically ill as a result of work-related stress.

b. **COVID-19-related stress is having a dramatic impact on employee productivity, and men appear to be disproportionately impacted.**

- 62% of workers reported losing at least one hour a day in productivity due to COVID-19 related stress, with 32% losing more than two hours per day.
- 70% of workers agreed that employees at their company are significantly less productive because of stress and anxiety surrounding COVID-19.
- Men are 27% more likely to lose hours of productivity. In fact, men report that their work lives are significantly more impacted by stress:

c. **Employees believe their company could do more to support their emotional and mental health.**

While 53% of workers said their company has increased its focus on employee mental health as a result of COVID-19, the research shows that there's room for improvement:

- 63% of workers reported that their company could do more to support their emotional and mental health during the COVID-19 pandemic. Within this group, 22 percent of workers said their company's response was "barely adequate", "a disaster" or "non-existent".
- Only 35% of people strongly agree that their employer is taking more of an interest in the emotional and mental health of employees now than in the past.
- 93% of employees believe that companies that survive COVID-19 will be those who support their employees' mental health.

"Companies that have strong emotional and mental health support for employees will be more likely to survive the impact of COVID-19"

d. **Employees were already interested in the virtual delivery of mental healthcare, and now they're quickly turning to it for support**

Before COVID-19, employees rated the ability to text or video chat with a mental health professional as the top service they desire from their mental health benefits - across almost all demographics including age, gender and role. Now, employees are rapidly turning to online solutions for support:

- 38% of employees have tried a technology-based mental health service. Of this group, 40% have tried it within the last week (3/25/20-4/1/20), 24 percent within the last month and 11 percent within the last 2 months.
- 70% of employees who used a technology-based mental health service for the first time in the past month did so to deal with COVID-19 stress. 48% tried it because their regular counsellor had moved to online sessions.
- 80% of employees would be more likely to use an emotional or mental health benefit if they access it through their smartphone.

As companies wrestle with business continuity planning, they must consider investing in mental health as a way to manage the dramatic increase in U.S. employee stress level and significant drop in productivity

It's crazy, but it's true: The havoc created by a virus on wellbeing is unimaginable; to have life turned around is crazy enough…let's explore what happens when a theory is now turned around on its head!

Chapter 2

Revisiting Maslow's Theory

"One's only rival is one's own potentialities. One's only failure is failing to live up to one's own possibilities. In this sense, every man can be a king, and must therefore be treated like a king."

Abraham Maslow

Introduction to Chapter 2

When we talk of Positivity at the Work Place, we always talk of a "Feel Good" factor! You can only feel good, if you believe you are good. You can only believe you are good, if you get the right signals and vibes that make you feel good. For this your basic needs and expectations need to be fulfilled, particularly in a work space arena.

Many leaders fall into the trap of focussing on the deliverables / task before building the relationships and focussing on the people in the team. (Wilson, n.d.)

"They create a 'task culture' which may well achieve early success, but a culture, that isn't sustainable in terms of high performance... Before long the team is in conflict, poor performance occurs and the team becomes affected by what is known as the 'dead body' syndrome. A terrible place where people come to survive and do the bare minimum. You have 'attendees' rather than 'high performers... As leaders we need to avoid the 'dead body' syndrome."

It is important to first understand and provide for team members before expecting them to deliver.

2.1 The Maslow's Theory of Motivation

What is needed can be understood by a well-known theory of motivation / needs. Although very old it still adds value into thinking about what you need to do... to lead a team and lends credence till today! NO Work space discussion starts or ends without Maslow's famous theory!

Maslow's Theory is proposed by Abraham Maslow in his 1943 paper "A Theory of Human Motivation" in Psychological Review. Maslow subsequently extended the idea to include his observations of humans' innate curiosity.

His hierarchy of needs is a motivational theory that comprises of a five-level model of human needs, represented by hierarchical levels within a pyramid. From the bottom of the pyramid, upwards, the needs are basic and going up towards more exalted ones: physiological, safety, love and belonging, esteem and self-actualization. He stated that the needs lower down in the hierarchy must be satisfied before individuals can attend to needs higher up the hierarchy.

Maslow's Theory of Motivation (Modified for Work space):

Consider this to be like a triangle with base being the broadest:

Level 1 (Base): Physiological Needs (Like Good air, Pure water, Clean fresh food, Sleep at Night, Clothing & Companionship)

Level 2: Safety Needs (Like safety on roads, Security at work, Safety at work, Job Security, Resources at work, Healthy work space, Own property)

Level 3: Love & Belonging (Like Attachment to work, friendship at Work, Sense of connection with colleagues, Family at Home)

Level 4: Esteem (Self-respect, Self Esteem, Status, Recognition at work, Strength of team, Freedom)

Level 5 (Top Of all): Self Actualisation (Desire to excel and flourish at work)

Maslow's Theory moves from Bottom to Up position, starting at the Base of the Triangle with Level 1.

Levels 1 and 2 are what are called as "basic needs" that are often presumed as ticked off! They are the basic pre-requisites and are taken as a Given in western cultures.

Levels 3 & 4 are called "Psychological needs" and are important for candidates at time of recruitment as well as those serving already in any work place.

Level 5 is different: It is a "Self-Fulfilment" need that when met, motivation to work increases. Work spaces aspire on improving motivation, consequently engagement and consequently productivity thru an increased focus on boosting the level 5 needs! This is a key attribute towards creating Positive work spaces.

As seen, Maslow divided the five needs into lower-level needs that were physical and high-level psychological needs. He proposed that if the low-level needs were met, individuals would focus on the high-level needs. In terms of a work environment, if a company meets an employee's basic needs for a comfortable workspace and job security, the employee is self-motivated to fulfil the higher-level needs. A company merely has to provide the opportunity to fulfil such needs by offering appropriate work.

If the employee can fulfil his high-level needs by working on a team, successfully completing a project and learning new skills in the course of carrying out the work, he can fulfil the three high-level needs and will be motivated to do the work well.

When building elite teams, most HR teams focus on making sure all these elements are met individually and people become the best versions of themselves.

High Performance Team Model

"When you combine the individual and teams needs that's when performance takes off. You'll really start driving your team towards success and achieve outstanding results as a leader. We need to create a place where everyone is striving to be the best they can be. Their physiological needs are met, they feel safe, loved, belong to something special, they are proud, confident and have high esteem. A place where the team has a purpose, goals are clear and values aligned. A place where spirit, skills, process and health all combine to ensure the magic happens." Says the paper by Wilson. (Wilson, n.d.)

To reach the top level of this motivational theory in the workplace, you must be self-actualized, which means you understand your skills, abilities and what you're capable of handling. A healthy and engaged workforce is filled with individuals who have reached the top level of Maslow's Hierarchy of Needs.

The ability to identify needs and fulfil them is the focus of most work spaces! When one feels safe, a sense of belonging and self-actualized, the Positive attitude also influences others around. Engagement and motivation are often team-based attitudes, so a team of individuals who feel their needs are being met can create a more positive, engaging culture within the workplace.

Funnily, Workplaces that have lesser Hierarchies meet more of the "Maslow's Hierarchy of needs"; conversely Hierarchical organisations that limit interaction and empowerment, reduce the meeting of the hierarchy of needs!

"To apply Maslow's concepts effectively, your organization has to specifically support fulfilment of the high-level needs. Design your company to allow social interactions that form the basis of a sense of belonging, acknowledge accomplishments to engender self-esteem and provide opportunities for employees to fulfil their potentials" (Wilson, n.d.).

2.2 Maslow Re-Visited (Post Pandemic)

With apologies to all work space theorists and to all avowed followers of Abraham Maslow, my theory re-visits the Way we read the Maslow's Pyramid of needs.

Post the Pandemic, things have changed; people have started talking less of Work Life balance and aspects of taking time out from work to discover themselves. Perhaps the world-wide lockdowns and the time out has allowed enough time to recoup and re-assess at a personal and spiritual level. Suddenly, what was the highest need on the chart of Hierarchy has become the base need or the starting point.

Level 1 (Base) has now become the Self Actualisation Need: almost a given and almost something that people feel has been sorted. If you have lasted in a job thru the Lockdown, its only because you are self-fulfilled and engaged with that job!

Level 2 & 3 now related to Self-esteem and Sense of Belonging. Wellness and Wellbeing at work, remains to be a mid-level need for Love, Belonging and Self-esteem; if anything, people have started missing the camaraderie and companionship and have resorted to virtual means of connecting in the pandemic; these erstwhile "Psychological needs" are now very much levels 2 and 3, well-watered with the increased emergence of connectivity virtually, if not physically.

Levels 4 & 5 are now the need for "Safety at work" and the need for "Pure Air, Sanitisation and Clean Food and water!" We may have called these the basics! Well, its back to the basics, then! The Base is now the TOP Most Need in the Hierarchy of Needs in the Post Pandemic Work place!

Do you see what's happening; we are slowly seeing a tectonic shift in the Maslow's Hierarchy of needs, post the Pandemic! What was level 1 is now Level 5 and what was level 5 is now Level 1. The Maslow's Triangle showing the Hierarchy of needs (at Work Post pandemic) now needs to be inverted!

The Triangle now stands on its tip with the Base representing the need of Self Actualisation at the lowest level moving upwards to the Top most level of need: Physiological Safety @ work.

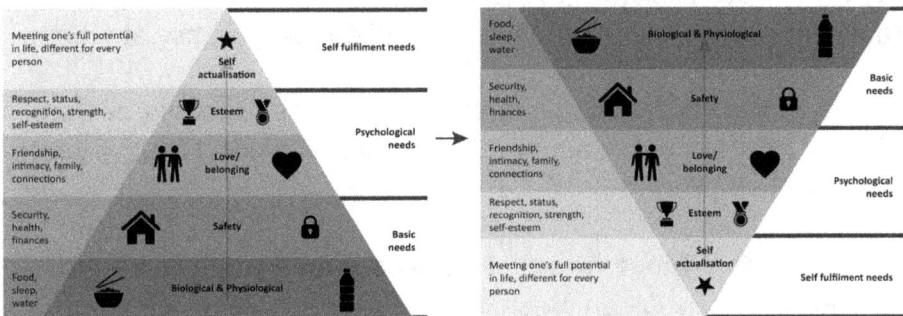

Earlier Maslow's Hierarchy of needs V/s Inverted Model (Post Pandemic)

The Post Pandemic Hierarchy of needs remains to be a five-level model of human needs, represented by hierarchical levels within a pyramid. But now its different; From the bottom of the pyramid, upwards, the needs are basic and going up towards more exalted ones: Self Esteem & Actualisation being basic, leading to love and "sense of belonging" (physiological needs) and then progressing to higher needs of safety, health and sanitisation.

It suddenly brings in the work place physicality as being the Most important aspect of a work place with renewed focus on health, safety, hygiene and wellbeing!

Maslow's Re-Visited Theory Suggested (Modified for Work space):

Consider this to be like a triangle that is now inverted and is on Tip:

Level 1 (Top Base need): Self Actualisation (Desire to excel and flourish at work)

Level 2: Esteem (Self-respect, Self Esteem, Status, Recognition at work, Strength of team, Freedom)

Level 3: Love & Belonging (Like Attachment to work, friendship at Work, Sense of connection with colleagues, Family at Home)

Level 4: Safety Needs (Like safety on roads, Security at work, Safety at work, Job Security, Resources at work, Healthy work space, Own property)

Level 5 (Top Most need): Physiological Needs (Like Good air, Pure water, Clean fresh food, Sleep at Night, Clothing & Companionship)

We suggest: Levels 1 and 2 are what are still continued to be called as "basic needs" relating to "Self-Fulfilment", that are now presumed as ticked off! Levels 3 & 4 are continued to be called "Psychological needs" and are important for candidates at time of recruitment as well as those serving already in any work place. Level 5 is NOW different: It is a need that when met, motivation to work increases.

Work spaces now can aspire to work on improving motivation, consequently engagement and consequently productivity thru an increased focus on boosting the level 5 needs: The Physiology / Physicality of the Work space: The Work Place in a new Avatar! This is a key attribute towards creating Positive work spaces.

2.3 The Post Pandemic Massive Change

The Inversion of the Triangle of the end user needs, is a Post pandemic Situation! What a Massive change in the way we look at the work space!

Covid has changed a lot of things!

Whilst a full chapter is devoted to these changing times, here is a brief look at some key changes worth mentioning upfront.

It has changed work place trends and systems that will have a far-reaching effect in the soon to be Post Pandemic World! There would-be Long-term changes such as:

THE MINDSET CHANGE

A new Post Pandemic Mindset would emerge, wherein a new order would need to be established, with the Employer no more a boss, but just a leader! People no more, just employees, but partners! Delegation replaced by Trust and Monitoring replaced by Self Discipline! Employee Management replaced by Process Planning & delegation!

DIGITAL TRANSFORMATION

The Pandemic has hastened a Digital Transformation that has speeded up a WFH approach that was always on the wish list of most employees! What has emerged is a Digital Landscape that has been accepted and applied as the new norm bringing in its wake reduced travelling, increased time spans for work and greater convenience! Furthermore, by adopting cloud-based operations, process automation, machine learning, most businesses will not only improve their functions but will also manage their costs better, boost productivity, and balance human and tech resources.

With greater Virtual and lesser Physical Interaction, there is a lot of self-reliance and independence in the work space thru this digital transformation that will change the work place densities for ever! Greater self-reliance would mean valuing every human more than ever before increasing sense of contribution, self-worth, esteem and self-actualisation!

The HUB & SPOKE Model

Offices will transform on account of this Digital transformation by adopting a "Neighbourhood Policy" of Distributed work! There would and could be more GIG Economy and work structures evolving with greater understanding and connectivity of people across different centres and geographical locations!

This would mean offices have greater Hot Seats and VC rooms than assigned seats of the past! Businesses and operations can and would expand to different regions with VC Connectivity! Businesses would become more independent and more stand alone; decentralisation instead of Consolidation would be the new Buzz Words! This would lead to greater diversity, independence and eventual productivity leading to Positivity!

Greater Inclusivity & Acceptance of WFH

The Increase self-reliant WFH typology has made a difference and broadened the catchment of resources by being more inclusive and more self-dependant work forces! The Work Model shall forever move to a more hybrid style which will be roster based on WFH & WFO in coming times, making people more independent. The New talk of Town is WFA: Work from Anywhere, more of which we shall focus on later!

Resimercial Approach

A New Phrase is doing the rounds: The "Resimercial Approach" which implies a more Residence Influenced Commercial Approach. Influenced from months of lockdown and the appreciation of a residential way of life, commercial establishments are increasingly bringing in a residential flavour to the work space! The shift is meant to lure people back to work spaces without having to make the adjustments too difficult.

While the past was more about "Working from Home", the post covid work space will look at "Homing from Work" and ensuring that the comforts and space index of homes influence the future work spaces.

Me replaces WE

With Greater time to spend with oneself and with lesser interaction with others physically, the pandemic has forever closed the argument of "Work Life Balance" that used to rage before the Pandemic.

With Greater time for "Introspection" and self-reflection, the "ME" has replaced the "WE"! Self-worth and self-appreciation are good at a unit level!

Previously a Group used to draw strength from the combine; now it is even stronger with stronger individual focus and responsibilities! Now a job assigned has got to be done on one's own rather than as a group, despite the many virtual platforms available in the virtual / digital world! In many ways "Resilience" and "Strength" have created a new confidence in each one of us: Makes for a more Positive ME!

2.4 The Post Pandemic Questions to Ask

Now that it's established the Maslow's Inverted triangle applies, it's important to know more of the organisation where the "People" work!

Designing a Work space that's positive is like solving a large Jigsaw Puzzle, where each piece of the puzzle has a precise piece of answer that needs to fit in to create a cohesive larger picture! The Nature of work has changed drastically in the last decade or so; it has changed un imaginably in the last year post the pandemic. Each industry had its own nuances; now each industry (post pandemic) has its own sub nuances in its way of getting work out of its people! Some have accepted the hybrid model, some have not; in either case, it's still a lot different from what it was before.

Therefore, what becomes complicated is that each project is like a different Jigsaw that needs to be solved individually.

Furthermore, just like in a Jigsaw puzzle, you need to have the vision of the entirety / entire work place for which It is essential to have a Holistic understanding of Three Questions:

1: WHO is the Client?

"WHO is the Client" entails understanding the background and the vocation of the client! Which Industry does he belong and what sort of team does he recruit or employ to meet his requirements! What is the age group and educational background of the teams and how is the organisation structured? What are the work hours, the work methodologies and the work types that are part of the requirement!? The more the end user typology is defined and directed, the clearer the solution becomes! The most difficult puzzles to solve are those that do not give you hints or clues! Often then designing appropriately is impossible, as it's akin to walking in the dark! Different answers to different aspects create different suitable responses to design for the user group! Definite answers to definite aspects create definite and defined responses in design!

It is because the "Who" is different in most projects, that the end solutions also need to be calibrated and hence a "one shoe fits all" policy does not work! Infact, here in lies the essence of sowing the seeds or originality;

because clients are different, the closer we understand them, the more different and varied are the appropriate solutions.

However, the industry needs to give more time and engagement to designers to be able to do justice to these critical understandings that direct the destiny of a project. Often that's not the case and that's the saddest part of work space design! Invariably, when time is compromised, architects need to draw out from their past experience and suppose that what they are doing will work for whom they are doing! It's like having to pull out a meal that's deep frozen in the refrigerator, microwave it and serve it as fresh food! The industry needs to understand that this is not a sustainable or viable way of working!

2: WHAT does The Client do?

"What does the client do" entails a deeper understanding of the nature of work of the client! Is the nature of work more outwardly or inwardly? Does he have to have external or internal meetings!? Definition of the public and private interface is critical. What is his external face and what is the internal face of the office!

Is the work domain into consulting or knowledge or imparting wisdom? Is the work domain more in the financial or technical arenas? Is this a service industry that is into support services like HR, recruitment, tele calling etc? Is the office a manufacturing or trading front office or a back office? Is this a media hub office or an insurance company?

Each typology has its own peculiarities that need to be researched into by understanding the work flows and nuances of the trade.

Departmental understanding is critical in governmental or semi-governmental organisations as also heavily Structured offices! Each department is in itself a mini subset office that feeds off the main office but retains its own existence and autonomy.

The "What" answer is like really knowing what cuisine the customer prefers, you cannot serve him veg or non veg meals! You need to know the unique dietary preferences of each department and serve accordingly.

This may seem simple on the face of it, but when the WHAT is avoided, there is a big void in understanding and applying the understanding of what really works for a client.

3: HOW does the client work?

The "How does he work" question is perhaps the most interesting of the three, as it requires deciphering and seeking answers to questions the client may not have even thought of!

Different clients have different ways of working; some require people to work in shifts and this entails needing lockers and spaces elsewhere to check into instead of desks. Some clients require their staff to work from defined contained areas only with little or no need for providing options, especially in ODCs, R&D offices and other restrictive work environments.

Some clients require the absolute opposite! They may need and embrace a more Agile and Activity based work approach which reflects in the way the seek the design to be! They may want to encourage greater collaboration and camaraderie for creating better and innovative solutions!

The clever question to ask is simply how do people work: do they work on laptops or desk tops? The answer often is a give-away on how mobile or free flowing should the work space be! The laptop has come to signify the modern office. The more mobile you are the more you can work from anywhere and this is what work space designers love to enquire!

All in all, a workspace architect or designer gets to work for a varied typology of client! Almost every client is unique in who he is and what he does! Thus, life is very interesting as the solutions need to be tailor made! One Recipe does not work for all!

The bottom line is that a good work space designer needs to be like a Specialised Chef! A Good Chef will come and ask you what you want and how you want it! He will customise the right meal for you and your individualistic taste! The idea is to serve "a la carte" instead of buffet meals that cater to all but satisfy few!

Chapter 3

Self-Fulfilment Needs @ Work

"There is short term happiness like bliss, joy and ecstasy, medium term happiness like satisfaction and well-being and long-term happiness like "finding what you are put on this earth for."

Stefan Sagmeister

The Happy Show Artist (Vrabie, 2013)

Introduction to Chapter 3

Chapter 2 Spoke about the "Inversion of the Maslow's Hierarchy of Needs Triangle" with inverted priorities from the based need of Self Actualisation to the Top need for Safety @ work place need.

Let's understand the Base need for happiness at Work, now: Self Actualisation / Fulfilment. There are many ways in which we understand what this really means? This chapter looks at Theories that make sense.

The Virtual world and way of working today ensures this (being a base question that needs to be answered). Today, there is no way somebody can feel attached to an organisation, working remotely, if he does not identify the work space goals with his! There is no way a virtual employee will work in a virtual employment if the Vision at a Self-level does not match that of the company!

And even if he does, just for the sake of the take home salary, his performance (or lack of it) would show up sometime or the other. Either he would make way or would be asked to make way for the next person in the line for the same job in today's VUCA world!

Let's study all that has been written about various theories that enhance work space productivity thru better fulfilment till now...

3.1 The PERMA Model

The PERMA Model, floated by Martin Seligman, a famous American Psychologist and Academician, mentions five key aspects to happiness and Positivity at the Work Place:

1. Positive Emotions (Feel Good factor)
2. Engagement (High Involvement)
3. Relationships (Connectivity)

4. Meaning (Sense of Purpose)
5. Accomplishments (Sense of Achievement)

According to Martin Seligman's research, the PERMA Model is very much applicable to the Work place, as it is here that we spend a big part of our day. We work with people who may not be friends and may at best be acquaintances or colleagues. It is true that the level of happiness experienced by each worker, as well as the work place environment, vastly affect the organization's productivity.

Therefore, the PERMA Model is one thing that should be applied in the workplace to foster a positive work environment that will eventually result in a happy and productive workforce (What is the PERMA Model?, n.d.)

Everything to do with The PERMA Model has been tested in the Pandemic Phase. This is either there or not there! Those who survived the Pandemic in the same place of work, had it. Those who did not, either left of their own volition or were asked...obviously displayed a lack of this.

Positive emotions / Feel Good factor (the Fundamental "P" of PERMA) could be thru that "intangible Glue" that keep us together even when we are not together at work: Work Place Culture! Work Culture is a very Big Word in Work space Design and is often the first thing to enquire into. We either feel good about being associated with our Work place or we do not! It's rarely 50:50. Much of this has to do with the work culture and the rest the Physical work space!

Similarly, **Engagement** & High Involvement at the work place is fundamental to creating a sense of self-esteem and feel-good factor. This can be thru making the work engaging and giving the right person, the right kind of work! It could also be allowing for engaging break out areas.

Relationships & Belongingness is basically creating a "sense of connectivity" between work place users & also self; while this may essentially be an HR Activity, it can also be created thru careful mix of collaboration areas across the office. The More the inter personal bond: the social skills with others, the better. But it's also the Intra personal bond: with one's own-self that is important! While Inter personal relates to one's personality and social skills, the intrapersonal skills relate to character & Self-management skills.

The sense of **Meaning** / Purpose for an organisation must align to personal value systems and be identifiable by the individual. Much has been said about this in the early chapters. In addition, CRS activities of the Work organisation can also create a sense of meaning and purpose in people's lives.

Accomplishments or a Sense of Achievement, or Acknowledgement, boost self-esteem and respect amongst teams. This needs to be fostered thru spreading of appreciation and creating an atmosphere of acknowledgement thru a Winners wall or Kudos wall to celebrate achievements and accomplishments.

Key Takeaways of this: (What is the PERMA Model?, n.d.)

When the PERMA Model is followed, there are higher chances of creating a happy workforce, which easily translates to a happy and productive workplace. Whether it is used by an individual as a tool for self-development or stress management or by a company to foster a positive working environment, the important thing is that each person's contribution is acknowledged.

3.2 The Ikigai & Golden Circle

While the origins of the Concept of Ikigai are Japanese and related to many centuries of belief, the fact is that it remains most relevant today, in the present-day world which has come to be known as the VUCA World (Volatile, Uncertain, Complex & Ambiguous); if anything, the Pandemic has made the world more VUCA than when the term was conceived!

Ikigai is thus the heart and core of the self. The New York Post Once quoted: "If *hygge* is the art of doing nothing, *ikigai* is **the art of doing something**—and doing it with supreme focus and joy."

Its premise is best described by a Japanese proverb: **"Only staying active will make you want to live a hundred years."**

As per the Los Angeles Times best seller Book **Ikigai: The Japanese Secret to a Long and Happy Life** (Garcia & Miralles, 2017) : *For the Japanese, everyone has an ikigai or a "reason for living". And according to the residents of the Japanese village with the world's longest-living people, finding it is the key to a happier and longer life. Having a strong sense of ikigai—the place where passion, mission, vocation, and profession intersect— means that each day is infused with meaning. It's the reason we get up in the morning. It's also the reason many Japanese never really retire*

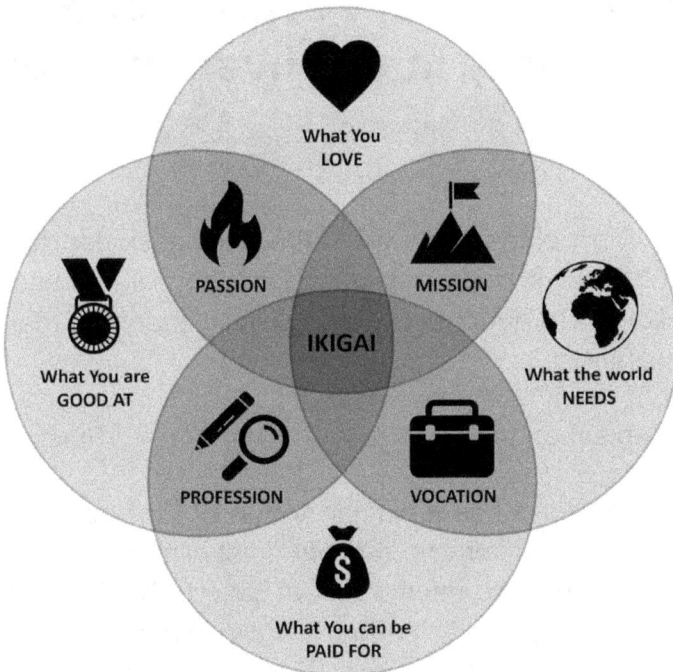

The Book is a highly recommended read and truly inspiring about how positivity and smile on the face can bring longevity and purpose to life.

At a personal level we have learnt that we need to find our Purpose in life: our MOJO or Our IKIGAI that lies at the intersection of our passion, our Skills and the demands of our industry! The Question is: Is our Work place really allowing us to find our MOJO? Does it allow us to instil a sense of Purpose and productivity in our lives that we seek!?

Does the Work place allow us to fire our passions, rather than dowse it? Does It hone our skills through collaboration? And does it allow us to better deliver our tasks in manners that benefit the organisation!

Every organisation also needs to have an Ikigai / Purpose.

The Western World has a similar notion of Purpose defined by acclaimed ted speaker and motivationist Simon Sinek, whom I personally follow, who uses a model called **The Golden Circle** to explain how legendary leaders like Steve Jobs, Martin Luther King Jr., and the Wright brothers were able to inspire, rather than manipulate, in order to motivate people. It is the framework for the WHY.

It needs to be able to ask and seek answers to questions famously called the Golden Circle by Simon Sinek! The Three Concentric Circles ask for an Organisation define its WHAT, HOW and WHY?

As Simon Sinek Says: "The More organisations and People who learn to start with WHY, the more people there will be who wake up being fulfilled by the work they do"

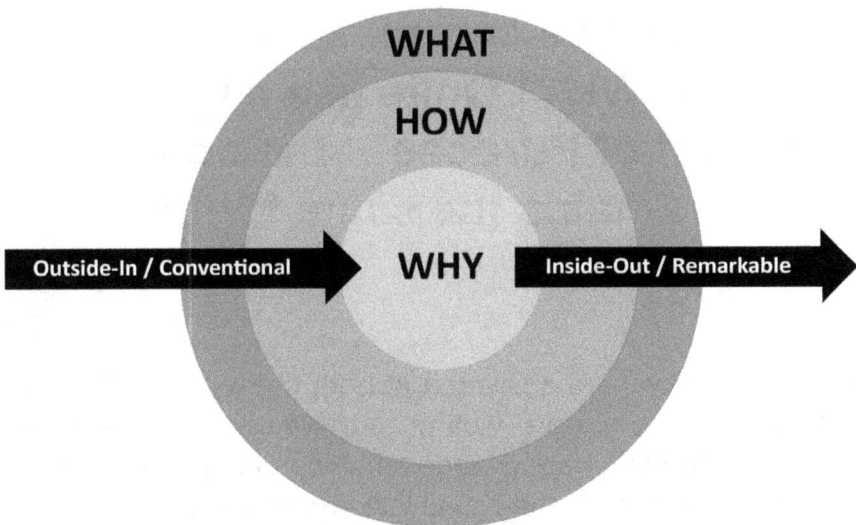

The Key Questions at any meaningful work place need to be:

- What are we doing as an organisation that sets us apart?
- How are we achieving our Vision, Mission and Goals?
- AND Most Importantly WHY are we doing what we are doing?

The Answer to WHY is the core "Mover and shaker" of people! Once you can get to the heart of the matter as why you want to do or achieve something, you can move people along with you... rather than just tell them what you want to do and how you want to! The Golden circle defines the priorities of the three "W's" with the bull's eye centre being the issue of WHY! Quite like Ikigai concept of Purpose... the core issue remains the same for the work place.

If these questions are answered at both the level of SELF and ORGANISATION, we are well on our way to happiness and Positivity! The First step towards an office being Positive, thus, lies at its core: It lies in the actual Vision, Mission and Goals that it sets out to follow and to make others who work there, follow!

3.3 The Importance of EQ (Emotional Quotient)

In an epic Book by Goleman titled "Emotional Intelligence – Why It Can Matter More Than IQ," published in 1995, it is well described how and why EQ is more important than IQ (Intelligence Quotient).

The Book describes five aspects of EQ

1. **Self-awareness**

   Self-Awareness: The extent to which one can understand their own and others, emotions is a main component of emotional intelligence. Self-awareness is the ability to recognize an emotion and its effects.

2. **Self-regulation**

   Self-regulation: The extent to which one can control their emotions and impulses. Self-regulation can avoid allowing negative emotions to lead to a long-term negative effect, i.e., not making impulsive, careless decisions, and thinking before they act.

3. **Motivation**

   Motivation: The extent to which one is able to motivate themselves to achieve their goals. Those who are motivated are achievement-driven, committed, optimistic, and take the initiative.

4. **Empathy**

   Empathy: The extent to which one is able to identify with and understand viewpoints of others. An empathetic person has a high level of emotional intelligence and is able to recognize the feelings of those around him / her even when those feelings may not be so apparent.

5. Social skills

Social Skills: The extent to which one is able to communicate with others and build and maintain relationships.

The more an individual is able to manage each of these areas, the higher their emotional intelligence is. Managers, are well known to need EQ more than IQ for successful team building and collaboration.

Emotional intelligence quotient (EQ) and intelligence quotient (IQ) are often mixed up concepts and need to be understood in the work place context, as both are important. **IQ** tests measure your ability to solve problems, use logic, and grasp or communicate complex ideas. **EQ** tests measure your ability to recognize emotion in yourself and others, and to use that awareness to guide your decisions

Hitherto, IQ was mostly considered to be the main "Determinant for Success". Soon, the concept of EQ (emotional quotient) was introduced as the new criteria for success. In fact, in the business world, many companies put in place mandatory emotional intelligence training and utilize emotional intelligence tests in the hiring process. Emotional intelligence is an important quality for business leaders and managers.

3.4 Concept of FLOW at the Work Place

Flow in the Workplace, is a concept floated by Positive psychologist Mihály Csíkszentmihályi, who describes flow as a state of complete immersion in an activity. It is further defined as a state of mind in which a person becomes fully immersed in an activity. While in this mental state, people are completely involved and focused on what they are doing. (Cherry, 2021)

> "The ego falls away. Time flies. Every action, movement, and thought follows inevitably from the previous one, like playing jazz. Your whole being is involved, and you're using your skills to the utmost," Csíkszentmihályi said in an interview with Wired magazine. (Gierland, 1996)

Flow experiences can occur in different ways for different people. It often occurs when you are doing something that you enjoy and in which you are quite skilled. Flow can also occur when workers are engaged in tasks where they are able to focus entirely on the project at hand. For example, a writer might experience this while working on a novel or a graphic designer might achieve flow while working on a website illustration.

How to Achieve Flow (Cherry, 2021):

So, what can you do to increase your chances of achieving flow? Ways to increase your chances of achieving flow:

- **Set clear goals**: In his book, Csíkszentmihályi explains that flow is likely to occur when an individual is faced with a task that has clear goals that require specific responses. A game of chess is a good example of when a flow state might occur. For the duration of a competition, the player has very specific goals and responses, allowing attention to be focused entirely on the game during the period of play.
- **Eliminate distractions**: It's more difficult to experience flow if there are things in your environment competing for your attention. Try reducing distracting things in your environment so you can fully focus on the task at hand.
- **Add an element of challenge**: "Flow also happens when a person's skills are fully involved in overcoming a challenge that is just about manageable, so it acts as a magnet for learning new skills and increasing challenges," Csíkszentmihályi explains. "If challenges are too low, one gets back to flow by increasing them. If challenges are too great, one can return to the flow state by learning new skills."
- **Choose something you enjoy**: You aren't likely to achieve flow if you are doing something you truly dislike. Focus on trying to achieve flow while working on something you love.

Achieving a state of flow can be a great way to make the activities you pursue more engaging and enjoyable. Not only do people often perform better when they are in this state of flow, but they are also often able to improve their skills in that area. Fortunately, it is also a skill you can learn to achieve with practice.

3.5 Self Determination Theory

Self Determination Theory offers a promising psychological theory of human well-being.

The theory emerged from empirical research into people's motivations and aspirations some 35 years ago and is still relevant to the day!

Self-determination theory grew out of the work of psychologists Edward Deci and Richard Ryan, who first introduced their ideas in their 1985 book *Self-Determination and Intrinsic Motivation in Human Behavior*. They developed a theory of motivation which suggested that **people tend to be driven by a need to grow and gain fulfilment.**

According to this Theory: People have several personal goals, but their achievement… does not always lead to higher well-being!

The research revealed that pursuing aspirations that lead to the satisfaction of three basic psychological needs would subsequently lead to high reported well-being, over the short-term and the long-term.

a. **Autonomy**: a feeling of choice and authenticity about our thoughts and behaviours.
b. **Competence**: a sense of efficacy and self-esteem, and a sense that we can have a meaningful impact on the world around us.
c. **Relatedness**: feeling that people care about us, and feeling close to others. More recent work has also floated a fourth psychological need – that for security.

The Self Determination Theory is a very important Aspect at the Work place, today as well. As per research paper (Cherry, Self-Determination Theory and Motivation, 2021) Self-determination is an important concept that refers to each person's ability to make choices and manage their own life.

This ability plays an important role in psychological health and well-being. Self-determination allows people to feel that they have control over their choices and lives. It also has an impact on motivation—people feel more motivated to take action when they feel that what they do will have an effect on the outcome.

Two key assumptions of the theory:

The need for growth drives behaviour. The first assumption of self-determination theory is that people are actively directed toward growth. Gaining mastery over challenges and taking in new experiences are essential for developing a cohesive sense of self.

Autonomous motivation is important. While people are often motivated to act by external rewards such as money, prizes, and acclaim (known as extrinsic motivation), self-determination theory focuses primarily on internal sources of motivation such as a need to gain knowledge or independence (known as intrinsic motivation).

Imagine a certain person who is unable to complete an important task at work. If he is high in self-determination, he will admit his fault and truly believe he can do something to fix the problem and correct the mistake.

But, If the same person is low in self-determination, he may, instead look for other things to blame. He could make excuses, assign blame, or refuse to admit that his own hand in them. And, it could be, that this person won't feel motivated to fix the problem. Instead, he may feel helpless to control the situation and believe that nothing will have any real effect.

Self-Determination in the Real World

Self-determination can play an important role in how people function in different aspects of their lives. Feeling in control and intrinsically motivated types of people, can feel more committed, passionate, interested, and satisfied with the things that they do.

People who feel that they are able to have a positive effect at work tend to feel more engaged and motivated. How else can employers build self-determination in their workers?

- Managers and leaders can foster this sense of self-determination by allowing team members to take an active role.
- Offer the team members responsibilities, provide meaningful feedback, and offer support and encouragement.
- Employers should be careful not to overuse extrinsic rewards. Too many rewards can undercut intrinsic motivation (the over justification effect); conversely, too few can cause employees to feel unappreciated.

Two Steps to improve your own sense of self-determination:

- Social connectivity is one of the main components of self-determination theory. Strong social relationships can foster motivation and well-being, while poor relationships can contribute to a poor sense of self and weak motivation.

- Becoming skilled in areas important to you, is a helpful way to build your sense of self-determination. Be it a strong interest in a hobby, sport, academic subject, or another area, learning as much as you can about it and improving your skills can help you feel more competent. The more you learn & practice, the more skilled and self-determined you will feel.

3.6 And Brief Theories…

The Following Concepts studied in great depth by a group of Work space Scientists (Vallina, Alegre, & Guerrero, 2018) shares and shows the factors relating to Positivity at the Work space:

Work context Factors:

Autonomy
Flexibility,
Supportive supervision,
Adequate staffing,
Workload management,
Environmental clarity,
Career development,
Situational factors,
Justice,
Feedback,
Empowerment,
Trust,
Dignified treatment,
Lean management,
Work climate,
Fair salary,
Perceived external social prestige,
Job resources

Leadership Factors: It helps when there are Good leaders!

Inspirational leadership,
Transformational leadership,
Transactional leadership,
Authentic leadership,
Creative leadership

Social interactions Factors:

Collaboration,
Interpersonal relationships,
High quality connections,
Workers and managers relationship,
Pleasant interactions,
Communication

Personal resources Factors:

Level of education,
Work family conflict,
Negative emotions,
Morale,
Time perspective,
Personal resources,
Resilience,
Authenticity,
Positive mood,
Proactive personality

The Conclusions from the paper (Vallina, Alegre, & Guerrero, 2018) drawn are interesting:

1. "We have explained the wide range of positive attitudes at work namely, job satisfaction, engagement, commitment, hedonia (happiness as pleasure) and **eudaimonia** (happiness as personal fulfilment), well-being,

psychological capital and happiness at work, to clarify the different aims and scopes."

2. "Second, our study reveals that in knowledge-intensive contexts, happiness at work depends mainly on work context factors, leadership styles, social interactions, and personal resources."

3. "Third, past research shows that promoting happiness at work is a worthy goal. The relationship between positive attitudes and performance has been defined as the 'Holy Grail' of research in organizational behaviour".

4. "A wider attitudinal measure should be developed to understand work behaviour, including job satisfaction, organizational commitment and other related constructs. Our research highlights the need for a broad-based, global measurement of happiness at work."

In conclusion, they say: the motivation of knowledge-intensive workers is a highly challenging task for many managers and academics. Accessing and retaining highly skilled knowledge-intensive workers is very competitive, because of the amount of value they add. Jobs where this type of employees can gain autonomy, communication and recognition seem to facilitate employees' happiness at work. Knowledge-intensive companies need worker commitment, satisfaction and engagement and therefore strategies must be focused on these areas. If the nature of a job is more challenging, with greater opportunities for growth and advancement, knowledge-intensive workers give their best to the organization, no matter how difficult the job is. Employment relationships are changing, the relationship between employers and employees needs to be strengthened, and happiness at work might be the clue for retaining the best employees in the future!

Paul J. Meyer is considered by many to be the founder of the self-improvement industry as it exists today. A celebrated trailblazer and leader of the multibillion-dollar self-improvement industry, Meyer says: "Productivity is never an accident; it is always the result of commitment to excellence, intelligent planning & focussed effort"

Chapter 4

Psychological Needs @ Work

The Mind is Everything. What you Think you become!

The Buddha

Introduction to Chapter 4

Whichever way you look at it, Pre Covid or Post Covid, Maslow's Hierarchy of needs scores "Psychological needs" centrally across both the Pyramids. Which means, whether in Pre pandemic or Post Pandemic Times, the need for Psychological happiness (Wellness & Wellbeing) is equally important.

The Mindset rules the rest of us. As they say: "Mindset is Everything".

A Mindset that focusses on wellness and wellbeing is positive in its outlook

The Most prolific amount of writing in recent times is on the Wellness and Wellbeing of The End Users in a Work space, as work spaces are where we spend most of our waking hours. The United Nations estimate a global average life expectancy of 72.6 years for 2019, which is approximately 636,000 days; of which 1/7th go in working at the desk! The Quality of the Work space then determines the Quality of our Lives!

The World Health Organization defines "Wellness as a state of complete physical, mental and social wellbeing, not just the absence of disease". However, for a lot of people, wellness means physical fitness, holistic care, happiness, relaxation, emotional balance, stress reduction, quality of life and spiritual health. ...

There is a lot of sameness in most minds about Wellness & Wellbeing; lets clarify: "Wellness" is a set of habits and behaviours, while "Well-being" is a state of mind. ... Wellness is more focused on physical health, while Well-being emphasizes mental and emotional health.

Many things affect wellness. There are eight aspects to your wellness. They are body, mind, environment, spirit, community, emotions, finances and work. Each can affect your quality of life.

How the do you Measure or Quantify Wellness and Wellbeing / Psychological happiness?

Well, the Following Sections have different organisations looking at different ways of rating Work space wellness that leads to overall positive mindsets! These start from looking at the Macro level down to the Micro levels: The City perspective to the Built Environment to the Contained Spaces via several filters / rating systems created already.

4.1 Ease of Living Index & World Happiness Report

Sometimes it's not just where you work, it's also where you live that makes a big difference, especially, when WFH has now become the new normal! The journey from "where you wake up from" to "where you work from" makes an impact on your sense of wellness and wellbeing.

The Two measures relate to the ease and happiness of living; very important to the measure of a positive frame of mind as you go to work every day, wherever you live!

The Ease of Living Index is a pre cursor to happiness at Work! Where you live, how you commute, how long it takes to offices, what Transport facilities are there (state sponsored or self) all make a difference on the Mindset of the Office-goer.

As I write, this morning's ET carries the ratings: "The ministry of housing and urban affairs on Thursday released the rankings of cities with a population of more than a million and a separate ranking for cities with population of less than a million. In the million plus cities, **Bengaluru**, Pune and Ahmedabad emerged as the most liveable cities of India. These were followed by Chennai, Surat, Navi Mumbai, Coimbatore, Vadodara, Indore and Greater Mumbai." (Sharma, 2021)

The EoLI is a measure of the Quality of Life in a city and its various parameters that entail the affordability of living, the sustainability factor of the city and the ability of a city to be resilient. It is also interesting to know that it is based on the citizens perception ratings as well.

The Citizen Perception Survey, in the index, holding a weightage of 30%, studies the existing living conditions through the lenses of **Quality of Life, Economic Ability, Sustainability**, spanning across 13 categories of:

- Education,
- Health,
- Housing and Shelter,
- WASH and SWM (Solid waste Management)
- Mobility,
- Safety and Security,
- Recreation,

- Level of Economic Development,
- Economic Opportunities,
- Environment,
- Green Spaces, and Buildings,
- Energy Consumption,
- and City Resilience,

(These account for 70% of the overall outcome.)

The reason these ratings are so interesting are that they are based on perceptions of the actual users in the city! Considering the city to be the larger landscape within which we work and live, its relevant how the large matrix is so meaningful to the human psyche at work!

"The methodology and approach for the revised edition of EoLI and MPI were released by MoHUA in February 2019. Essentially, the EoLI report aims to measure the well-being of Indian citizens in 111 cities, across the pillars of Quality of Life, Economic-ability, and Sustainability, with 49 indicators under 13 categories. The EoLI primarily seeks to accelerate India's urban development outcomes, including the achievement of the Sustainable Development Goals. The findings from the index can help guide evidence-based policymaking. It also promotes healthy competition among cities, encouraging them to learn from their peers and advance their development trajectory." (Bureau, 2021)

Separately, at a Global level, the **World Happiness Report** is a publication of the United Nations Sustainable Development Solutions Network. It contains articles and rankings of national happiness, based on respondent ratings of their own lives, which the report also correlates with various (quality of) life factors. As of March 2020, Finland was ranked the happiest country in the world… three times in a row

While Finland, Denmark, Switzerland and Iceland are the happiest spaces on earth, India ranks a low 144 out of 156 countries surveyed, according to a recent UN report.

4.2 Ease of Doing Business

Published by the World Bank, The Ease of Doing Business Index, is an aggregate figure that includes different parameters which provide an indication of how easy is doing business in a country.

It is calculated by Adding the **"distance to frontier scores"** of different economies. The **distance to frontier score** captures the gap between an economy's performance and a measure of best practice across the entire sample of 41 indicators for 10 Doing Business topics.

The distance to frontier score uses the 'regulatory best practices' for doing business as the parameter and benchmark economies according to that parameter.

Its important to know that for each of the indicators forming a part of the statistic 'Ease of doing business,' a distance to frontier score is computed and all the scores are aggregated. The aggregated score, then, becomes the Ease of doing business index.

"Indicators for which distance to frontier is computed include construction permits, registration, getting credit, tax payment mechanism etc. Countries are ranked as per the index." (Definition of 'Ease Of Doing Business', 2021)

INDIA – EASE OF DOING BUSINESS RANKING

Among the chosen 190 countries, India ranked 63rd in Ease of Doing Business 2020: World Bank Report. In 2014, the Government of India launched an ambitious program of regulatory reforms aimed at making it easier to do business in India. The program represents a great deal of effort to create a more business-friendly environment.

India has emerged as one of the most attractive destinations not only for investments but also for doing business. India jumps 79 positions from 142nd (2014) to 63rd (2019) in 'World Bank's Ease of Doing Business Ranking 2020'. (Unknown, Ease of Doing Business, n.d.)

The ease of doing business index is made to measure regulations directly affecting businesses and not for more general conditions such as a nation's proximity to large markets, quality of infrastructure, inflation, or crime.

The next step of gathering data surveys of over 12,500 expert contributors (lawyers, accountants, etc.) in 190 countries who deal with business regulations in their day-to-day work. These individuals interact with the *Doing Business* team in conference calls, written correspondence, and visits by the global team. For the 2017 report, team members visited 34 economies to verify data and to recruit respondents. Data from the survey is subjected to several rounds of verification. The surveys are not a statistical sample, and the results are interpreted and cross-checked for consistency before being included in the report. Results are also validated with the relevant government before publication. Respondents fill out written surveys and provide references to the relevant laws, regulations, and fees based on standardized case scenarios with specific assumptions, such as the business being located in the largest business city of the economy. (Ease of Doing Business Index, n.d.)

A nation's ranking on the index is based on an average of 10 subindices:

1. Starting a business – Procedures, time, cost, and minimum capital to open a new business
2. Dealing with construction permits – Procedures, time, and cost to build a warehouse
3. Getting electricity – procedures, time, and cost required for a business to obtain a permanent electricity connection for a newly constructed warehouse
4. Registering property – Procedures, time, and cost to register commercial real estate
5. Getting credit – Strength of legal rights index, depth of credit information index
6. Protecting investors – Indices on the extent of disclosure, the extent of director liability, and ease of shareholder suits
7. Paying taxes – Number of taxes paid, hours per year spent preparing tax returns, and total tax payable as a share of gross profit
8. Trading across borders – Number of documents, cost, and time necessary to export and import
9. Enforcing contracts – Procedures, time, and cost to enforce a debt contract
10. Resolving insolvency – The time, cost, and recovery rate (%) under a bankruptcy proceeding

The Doing Business project also offers information on the following datasets:

- Distance to the frontier – Shows the distance of each economy to the "frontier," which represents the highest performance observed on each of the indicators across all economies included since each indicator was included in *Doing Business*

- Entrepreneurship – Measures entrepreneurial activity. The data is collected directly from 130 company registrars on the number of newly registered firms over the past seven years
- Good practices – Provide insights into how governments have improved the regulatory environment in the past in the areas measured by *Doing Business*
- Transparency in business regulation – Data on the accessibility of regulatory information measures how easy it is to access fee schedules for 4 regulatory processes in the largest business city of an economy

4.3 Great Places to Work

Beyond all the state sponsored certifications and ratings mentioned above, it's good to know that there are many private Sector initiatives and certification bodies that define and recognise Positivity in Work Places that help organisations, not just design and process but also "run" Good Work Places!

The key to creating a great workplace was not a prescriptive set of employee benefits, programmes, and practices, but the building of high-quality relationships in the workplace — relationships characterised by trust, pride, and camaraderie.

These relationships were not a "soft" activity, but key drivers that help improve an organisation's business performance.

The mission role of trust in the workplace became core, not only for that first, pioneering 1984 book, but its 1988 sequel, "A Great Place to Work: What makes some employers so good – and most so bad." These insights led to the founding of Great Place to Work® Institute.

Business leaders, globally, adopted the Institute's models and methodology as a valuable way to measure and create "Great Workplaces". In 1997, FORTUNE partnered with the Institute's research arm to produce the world's first 100 Best Companies to Work For workplace rankings. Great Place to Work® gradually opened doors in more than 60 countries around the world with more growth slated in the coming years.

Certain criteria developed by Great Places to Work's Tabitha Russel Wilhelmson (WILHELMSEN, 2019):

a. *Hiring: What characteristics do you look for in new employees? (Why it matters: Because companies that care about their cultures are extraordinarily selective in who they hire, and attend to a candidate's skill set and culture fit. Hiring practices will include opportunities to engage the candidate with many different people in the company, and clearly tie in with the organization's culture, values, and mission.)*

b. *Welcoming: How do you welcome new employees and integrate them into your culture? (Why it matters: Because great workplaces use distinct and varied methods of giving all new hires a warm welcome, integrating them into the culture from Day One.)*

c. *Inspiring: How do you inspire employees to feel that their work has meaning? (Why it matters: Because at organizations with great cultures, employees feel connected to a shared purpose when they come to work each day. Programs are in place that help foster pride, and show employees the value of their work for customers and for society overall.)*

d. **Speaking: What are distinctive ways senior management shares information, including bad news?** *(Why it matters: Because leaders at great workplaces understand the important role that sharing information plays in maintaining a trust-based relationship with employees. Transparency, accessibility and warmth are all aspects we see incorporated into information sharing at the Best.)*

e. **Listening - Upward Communication: How can employees ask questions, provide feedback, or otherwise communicate with managers, especially senior managers?** *(Why it matters: Because just as being informed is an important component of trust-building, so is offering employees the opportunity to ask questions of leaders. Organizations scoring highly on this question demonstrate a sincere interest in hearing employee feedback, and offer a variety of methods for doing so.)*

f. **Talking – Collaborating/Innovation: How do you encourage all employees to share new ideas and better ways of doing things? How have these efforts have translated into positive improvements and innovations for your business and people?** *(Why it matters: Because tapping into the insights of employees, particularly those that work on the front line, helps create an Innovation by All culture, where employees feel motivated and inspired to come up with the next great idea that will benefit the organization and its bottom line.)*

g. **Thanking: How does your company show appreciation and/or recognition for employees' good work and extra effort, or other achievements?** *(Why it matters: Because when employees are appreciated for their work, they know that they are valued and respected as* *an important part of the organization. Great workplaces embrace a culture of appreciation, and offer a variety of programs that give all employees that opportunity to be frequently recognized.)*

h. **Developing: How does your company help employees discover and develop their talents, challenge themselves professionally, manage their careers, and/or enhance their personal growth?** *(Why it matters: Because when leaders value their employees as a critical part of the company's success, they treat training and development as a top priority. Great workplaces foster a culture of learning, and provide all employees a variety of channels to further both their professional growth and personal interests.)*

i. **Caring - Balancing: In what distinctive ways does your company help employees balance their work lives with their personal and/or family lives? How do you support employees during significant live events (such as a personal crisis, family illness, birth, marriage, etc.)?** *(Why it matters: Because great workplaces make it clear that they care for employees as full human beings—not just as employees. These organizations provide a range of work/life benefits and programs that all employees have access to, and that support a wide variety of individual needs.)*

j. **Caring - Including: How do you ensure you are creating a great workplace for all employees regardless of their personal backgrounds and place in the organization? Do you have programs and/or policies intended to promote diversity and/or inclusion across personal demographics and job roles?** *(Why it matters: Because truly great workplaces are great for everyone who works there, showcasing a variety of programs and practices that foster a diverse workforce and promote inclusion at all levels.)*

k. **Celebrating: How do you encourage fun and camaraderie among your employees?** *(Why We Ask: Because great workplaces understand that camaraderie* *and fun are essential to great culture, and find many excuses to have fun and celebrate.)*

l. **Sharing - Rewards: What is your company's approach to financially compensating employees? What are the methods used to determine levels of compensation? Do you have unique or special forms of compensation (i.e. profit sharing, bonuses, etc.)? What policies and/ or practices do you have that promote a sense of equity between employees and managers?** *(Why it matters: Because great workplaces focus efforts on ensuring that their compensation-related activities are fair, well-communicated, and inclusive.)*

m. **Sharing - Community: What are your organization's philanthropic, environmental, or other corporate social responsibility initiatives, and how do employees participate in and/or derive value from these efforts?** *(Why it matters: Because great workplaces demonstrate a sense of care that extends beyond their immediate workforce and customers. Such organizations have a variety of philanthropic programs and practices that they actively encourage employees to participate in, and that often tie into the mission and values of the company.)*

n. **Leadership Effectiveness: What is your executive team's current short and long-term strategy and philosophy for ensuring a successful business? What was the process for developing it, and how was it communicated across all levels of the business?** *(Why it matters: It's not enough to have a solid strategy to ensure business success – great workplaces also involve employees in developing this strategy, and make a conscious effort to reinforce the strategy across all lines of business, ensuring employees can connect their daily work to the overarching goals of the organization, which makes them feel valued and inspired.)*

Organisations that create great workplace culture for their employees, perform better. Remember the "WHY" is the Most important part of the discussion!

Here are some of the reasons WHY Organisations like to Certify themselves as GREAT PLACES TO WORK:

- Attract Retain Talent
- Customer Centric Mindset
- Growing Bottom Line
- Agility & Speed
- Develop Culture of Innovation
- Professional Excellence
- Project Your Employer Brand Externally
- Earn National Recognition

Great Place to Work® Certification is the most definitive 'Employer-of-Choice' recognition that organizations aspire to achieve. This Certification is recognized globally by employees and employers alike and is considered the 'Gold Standard' in identifying and recognizing Great Workplace Cultures.

Every year, more than 10,000 organizations across 60 countries apply to get Great Place to Work–Certified. The participating organizations are assessed through two lenses and, on meeting the qualifying criteria, are

Certified as a Great Place to Work for a period of 1 year. The two lenses are called Trust Index© and Culture Audit©

The new model of a **Great Place To Work FOR ALL**, builds on the Trust Model by ensuring that everyone irrespective of their job role, tenure, age or gender at the Best Workplaces is having a consistently positive experience. Great workplaces FOR ALL are able to maximize their human potential through effective leaders, meaningful values, and a deep foundation of trust with all employees, regardless of who they are or what they do for the organisation. Companies that have succeeded in creating great workplaces FOR ALL benefit from improved innovation and sustained financial growth.

- **Values** – Company values are not just what's written on the walls or website, but what employees actually experience in their day-to-day work lives, particularly in how they see their leaders.
- **Leadership Effectiveness** – An effective leadership team has an emotional connection with their company's culture and its people, as well as an ability to create a coherent and effective strategy at every level of the business
- **Maximizing Human Potential** – A great workplace for everyone regardless of who you are or what you do in your company.
- **Innovation By All** – A culture that enables a company to continuously improve, adapt quickly and generate pivotal opportunities by tapping into the intelligence, skills, and passion of everyone in the organization.
- **Financial growth** is an outcome of great workplaces

Many organisations having impressive programs on paper, in practice don't see the benefits of these investments in spite of hefty investments in those programs. Great Place to Work has found there are five underlying qualities that magnify the success of best company suites of programs: their **variety, originality, all-inclusiveness, degree of human touch, and integration with the culture at large.** (Great Place To Work Model, n.d.)

Great Places to work pride themselves on Credibility, Respect, Fairness, pride & Camaraderie.

4.4 GRIHA Norms

GRIHA is an acronym for "Green Rating for Integrated Habitat Assessment".

Actually, GRIHA is a Sanskrit word that means 'Abode'.

Human Habitats (buildings) interact with the environment in various ways. Throughout their life cycles, from construction to operation and then demolition, they consume resources in the form of energy, water, materials, etc. and emit wastes either directly in the form of municipal wastes or indirectly as emissions from electricity generation. GRIHA attempts to minimize a building's resource consumption, waste generation, and overall ecological impact to within certain nationally acceptable limits / benchmarks.

Going by the Famous Peter Drucker Quote 'what gets measured, gets managed', GRIHA

attempts to quantify aspects such as energy consumption, waste generation, renewable energy adoption, etc. so as to manage, control and reduce the same to the best possible extent.

GRIHA is a rating tool that helps people assesses the performance of their building against certain nationally acceptable benchmarks. It evaluates the environmental performance of a building holistically over its entire life cycle, thereby providing a definitive standard for what constitutes a 'green building'. The rating system, based on accepted energy and environmental principles, will seek to strike a balance between the established practices and emerging concepts, both national and international.

Today, buildings have evolved into a diverse array of typologies designed to meet the highly specific requirements of the people who live and work in them. Over time, with growing technological skills, these buildings have also been increasingly designed and operated to place exorbitant demands on natural resources, such as land, water, and energy, to mention a few. Therefore, incorporation of sustainable practices in building design and operation is no longer a choice but a necessity for a sustainable future. (GRIHA Rating, n.d.)

The GRIHA v.2015 has undergone an extensive revision to account for the ongoing advancements in the highly dynamic construction sector. This version (i.e. GRIHA v2019) integrates concepts like life cycle cost analysis, life cycle analysis, and water performance index to name a few. This version has taken into consideration the incorporation of user experience, market feedback, and enhanced ease of implementation and adoption.

GRIHA v.2019

Section	Criterion No.	Criterion Name	Maximum Points
1. Sustainable Site Planning	1	Green Infrastructure	5
	2	Low Impact Design	5
	3	Design to Mitigate UHIE	2
2. Construction Management			
	4	Air and Soil Pollution Control	1
	5	Top Soil Preservation	1
	6	Construction Management Practices	2
3. Energy Efficiency	7	Energy Optimization	12
	8	Renewable Energy Utilization	5
	9	Low ODP and GWP Materials	1
4. Occupant Comfort	10	Visual Comfort	4

	21	Alternative Materials for External Site Development	2
8. Life Cycle Costing	22	Life Cycle Cost Analysis	5
9. Socio-Economic Strategies	23	Safety Sanitation for Construction Workers	1
	24	Universal Accessibility	2
	25	Dedicated Facilities for Service Staff	2
	26	Positive Social Impact	3
10. Performance Metering and Monitoring	27	Commissioning for Final Rating	7
	28	Smart Metering and Monitoring	0
	29	Operation and Maintenance Protocol	0
		Total Points	**100**
11. Innovation	30	Innovation	5
Grand Total Points	**100 + 5**		

The benefits

And while these parameters benefit the community at large with the improvement in the environment by reducing Green House Gas emissions, reducing energy consumption and the stress on natural resources, it al;so makes for a more positive work environment.

Working in such buildings allows for a conscious statement of purpose and increased engagement and productivity! When well marketed, this also makes for enhanced image and marketability and sense of pride!

4.5 LEEDS Ratings

On the Global level, here is the more popular rating system on the planet: The LEED (Leadership in Energy and Environmental Design) is the most widely used green building rating system in the world. Available for virtually all building types, LEED provides a framework for healthy, highly efficient, and cost-saving green buildings.

Projects pursuing LEED certification earn points for various green building strategies across several categories based on the number of points achieved, a project earns one of four LEED rating levels: Certified, Silver, Gold or Platinum. Learn more.

The LEED® rating system has seven areas of concentration; Sustainable Sites, Water Efficiency, Energy and Atmosphere, Materials and

Resources, Indoor Environmental Quality, Innovation in Design Process and Regional Priority. Projects obtain credits in these areas to achieve certification.

A building becomes certified after receiving a minimum of 40 credits from the USGBC.

LEED® Certification Levels

LEED® Certified	40 – 49 points
Silver Level	50 – 59 points
Gold Level	60 – 79 points
Platinum Level	80 + points

The point distribution over the seven categories are as follows:

Category	Available Points
Sustainable Sites	26
Water Efficiency	10
Energy and Atmosphere	35
Materials and Resources	14
Indoor Environmental Quality	15
Innovation in Design	6
Regional Priority	4
Total Possible Points	110

What LEEDS does is that it ensures a Built environment is made to enable reduction in Operating costs ranging from 30% savings for Silver rated buildings to 48% for Gold rated ones to 50-60% savings for Platinum rated ones. Money saved, they say, is Money earned and allows for better use of saved funds for employee welfare!

There is also upgradation of the IAQ (Indoor Air Quality) and sense of wellness and wellbeing in a LEEDS certified Building!

LEEDS also creates VALUE: it typically allows for 20% increase in lease rates for CLASS A CRE. Sometimes, the building you are moving to, also makes the difference in the VIBE for the Work space!

4.6 Well Standards

Having discussed LEEDS, it is often asked what is the difference between LEEDS and WELL standards? The Answer is simple: LEEDS focuses on "Buildings & The Built Environment"; Well Standards focus on "People".

While Both were programs started by the USGBC (U.S. Green Building Council), LEEDS started in 1998 while WELL began in 2014. As per detailed paper written (Watt, 2019), the WELLNES concerns centre around:

Now, let's take a look at WELL. In order to be WELL certified, a facility must meet seven criteria, or "concepts," in WELL program terminology:

1. *Air: While Typically, a facility have two indoor air quality checks; one before it is occupied and the second after it has been occupied for several months, it does not always happen. The WELLS process is designed to ensure that healthy indoor air quality is maintained once the facility is*

fully operational. To accomplish this, the WELL program requires that building windows are operational (can open and close); no smoking is allowed in the facility; all building finishes and interiors are selected so that they meet strict standards about off-gassing; and the cleaning solutions used to maintain the facilities are not only green-certified but release few if any volatile organic compounds (VOCs).

2. ***Water:*** *Potable (drinking) water used in the facility must be filtered, once again meeting specific standards. It cannot be hard and must not contain suspended soils, dissolved materials, chlorine, or fluoride.*

3. ***Nourishment:*** *Don't expect to find chips and cookies in the vending machines of a WELL certified building. Instead, vending machines (and all food offerings) are to be healthier food options such as 100 percent organic fruit, vegetables, as well as low-fat grab-and-go foods. Meat or chicken food items, if they are available, must be both hormone-and-antibiotic free and vegetarian fed.*

4. ***Light:*** *While the LEED program does encourage the use of daylighting, it does so mainly to reduce energy consumption. With the WELL program, light must ensure "good visual acuity when performing a variety of tasks to avoid eyestrain and to minimize productivity losses and headaches."*

5. ***Fitness:*** *Most likely you figured this would be part of the WELL program. While the program does not necessarily require that a gym be included in a facility, it certainly can help. What the standard does entail is that the building provides users with "the ability to carry out daily tasks with vigor and alertness, without undue fatigue, and with ample energy to enjoy leisure-time pursuits and respond to emergencies." This requirement can be accomplished by providing a fitness center, bike and walking paths, or encouraging staff to use stairs instead of the elevator, as well as providing shower areas for building users.*

6. **Comfort:** *A common problem in the work environment is noise. In order to be WELL certified, steps must be taken to sound insulate facilities, protecting users from both outside as well as inside noise. Further, if needed, the facility must provide personal humidifiers, fans, standing desks, and adjustable desks.*
7. **Mind:** *This is a rather broad "concept." One WELL certified building housing a landscaping company tackled this concept by installing an online library and resource center. The resource center provided books, articles, graphics, and other information designed to stimulate ideas and help the staffers perform their duties.*

As per Research (Watt, 2019) by 2019, there have been more than 1,610 WELL projects, resulting in 159 certifications and 1,451 registered projects, which refers to facilities in the process of being WELL certified. We should also point out that this is an international program. The WELL "community" is now found in 81 countries and includes nearly 8,000 associated professionals worldwide helping facilities around the world become WELL certified.

As per the Well Web site (unknown, Well Building Standard, 2020) WELL is composed of over one hundred Features that are applied to each building project, and each WELL Feature is designed to address issues that impact the health, comfort, or knowledge of occupants.

Many WELL Features intended to improve health are supported by existing government standards or other standards-setting organizations. Some Features are intended to change behaviour through education and corporate policy or culture, and provide information and support for making positive lifestyle choices.

WELL Features can be:

- Performance-based standards: allow flexibility in how a project meets acceptable quantified thresholds.
- Descriptive standards: require that specific technology, design strategies, or protocols are implemented.

WELL standards can be applied across diverse CRE sectors, with the current WELL v1 being optimized for "commercial and institutional office" buildings.

4.7 Wellness & Wellbeing

Moving from Well Standards to "Wellness & Wellbeing" its important to mention: Well, they are not the same! Both relate to people, but Wellness is more individual!

Susie Ellis, (Institute, 2016) suggest that "wellness gets firmly associated with health and prevention, and well-being becomes more associated with happiness". The reason? People are beginning to pay more attention to "indexes," such as the Gallup-Health ways "Well-Being Index" and the UN's "World Happiness Report," and are finding that happy countries aren't necessarily healthy countries. Nor are healthier countries necessarily happy ones.

In this shift in paradigm (Unknown, Key Concepts & Shared Language, 2018), wellbeing refers to a more holistic approach to health by including the presence of positive emotions and moods, the absence of negative emotions, and satisfaction with life, fulfilment and positive functioning.

More simply, wellbeing can be referenced as a holistic "whole-of-life" experience consisting of judging life positively and feeling good while wellness refers to the active process through which people become aware of, and make choices toward, a more successful existence.

John Valenty, (CEO Wellness.com) best describes this: "Wellness is the result of personal initiative, seeking a more optimal, holistic and balanced state of health and well-being across multiple dimensions."

Promoting wellbeing can help prevent stress and create positive working environments where individuals and organisations can thrive. Good health and wellbeing can be a core enabler of employee engagement and organisational performance.29-Apr-2020.

As per research done (Unknown, Wellness vs. Wellbeing Programs: What's the difference?, 2018) *"53% of businesses with wellbeing initiatives experienced improved employee engagement and satisfaction."*

This is an eye-opening statistic.

Wellness Dimensions

Wellness involves the awareness of our current state of health in multiple dimensions with the initiative, tools and support to make lasting changes towards a more optimal life. The primary top-level dimensions of wellness are:

Mental Wellness

- The mental dimension of wellness includes developing a healthy personal philosophy, maintaining a learning aptitude and establishing a base of useful knowledge.

Physical Wellness

- The physical dimension of wellness includes our overall physical health, physical fitness and appearance. This includes Good Indoor Air Quality, Low VOC Materiality, Good Sound Acoustics, Good Lighting & Good Thermal Comfort.

Spiritual Wellness

- The spiritual dimension of wellness includes becoming aware of our life's purpose, developing our innate gifts and using our talents in a positive way and getting in touch with our spirituality. Operating "on purpose" and using our talents can be spiritually lifting and tremendously positive as compared to merely getting by, pleasing others, or surviving.

Social Wellness

- The social dimension of wellness includes the careful creation and maintenance of healthy and positive relationships, Social Connectivity (interpersonal & intra-personal) and a sense of Mindfulness.

Lifestyle Wellness

- The lifestyle dimension of wellness includes our work and workplace, our leisure time and our home environment. Access to good Nourishment, safe drinking water, beverages etc add to a sense of wellbeing like nothing else does!

The main aspects of individuals' working lives and their implications in terms of best practise to foster well-being at work are summarised below, structured according to the dynamic model of well-being. (Jeffrey, Mahoney, Michaelson, & Abdallah, 2021)

A. Personal resources (Health & Vitality; Work Life balance)
B. Organisational System (Fair Pay; Job Security; Job Clarity; Appraisal Management System; Work Environment; Social Value)
C. Functioning At Work (Using Strengths and having sense of progress; Sense of Control; Work relations)
D. Experience of Work (Positive & Negative feelings)

The Most fascinating research from Forbes (Beheshti, 2019) suggests 10 Timely statistics about connection between Employee Engagement & Wellness:

1. Highly engaged teams show 21% greater profitability
2. 89% of HR leaders agree that ongoing peer feedback and check-ins are key for successful outcomes

3. Employees who feel their voice is heard are 4.6 times more likely to feel empowered to perform their best work
4. 96% of employees believe showing empathy is an important way to advance employee retention
5. Disengaged employees cost U.S. companies up to $550 billion a year
6. 61% of employees are burned out on the job
7. 89% of workers at companies that support well-being initiatives are more likely to recommend their company as a good place to work
8. 70% of employers have improved their physical environments to encourage healthy behaviors
9. 61% of employees agree that they have made healthier lifestyle choices because of their company's wellness program
10. 87% of employees expect their employer to support them in balancing work and personal commitments

So, all that has been said in this chapter, creates a platform for a Positive Mindset that makes it possible to bring in the positivity that's needed at a Psychological level at the work place.

Its now over to the Physicality of the space and its Physiology that would help complete the happiness at workplace phenomenon.

Chapter 5

Basic Needs 1: Better Work Space "Design Process"

5.1 Understand (Context is Everything & Client is King)

5.2 Plan (Planning is the priority)

5.3 Layer

5.4 Enable

5.5 The X Factor

The 30 Points Work Spaces Design Checklist: UPLEX

"The role of the designer is that of a good, thoughtful host anticipating the needs of his guests."

–Charles Eames

Introduction to Chapter 5

Chapter 2 introduced the concept of this book: Inverting the Maslow's Hierarchy of Needs in a Post pandemic World, to make "Basic needs of Self actualisation and Fulfilment" be base level needs, as explained in chapter 3. Further the "Psychological needs" were mid-tier expectations and explained in the previous Chapter 4.

It's now time to understand relate to what the changed perception of the TOP Need: "The Physiological needs" of a work place are today! "How and why are work spaces relevant" will be a debate that will start but never end; in the interim how can we design our work spaces more scientifically in a more structured way? We talk all about that!

As per a study paper by Chloe Taylor "56% of workers ranked a strong workplace culture as more important than salary." (Taylor, 2019)

He Further adds that "A common misperception among many employers today is that pay and work-life balance are among the top factors driving employee satisfaction... Instead, employers looking to boost recruiting and retention efforts should prioritize building strong company culture and value systems, amplifying the quality and visibility of their senior leadership teams and offering clear, exciting career opportunities to employees."

Building a GOOD work culture: is all about creating happiness at the work place, that makes all the difference (Whalen, 2020)

Improved Productivity

Research shows that a happy workplace results in a 12% increase in employee productivity. Conversely, unhappy workers are 10% less productive than workers reporting average levels of workplace satisfaction. A positive environment creates employees who perform better, exceed expectations, achieve goals, are self-motivated, and work more efficiently.

Enhanced Creativity

When employees are less anxious at work, they come up with better ideas, better solutions to problems, greater innovations and greater participation n brainstorming. All in all, this means greater Engagement & Creativity at work.

Improved Health

Employee absenteeism, due to stress related issues at work, do cost organizations greater money by reducing productivity, driving up the cost of health insurance, and decreasing turnover. Statistics show that an absent employee could cost $16,000 keeping in mind the costs towards recruitment, training, and opportunity losses. The reverse happens and organizations benefit, when employees work and show greater zeal and energy.

Increased Loyalty

Contented and health workforces create a band of loyalists willing to go the extra mile for the team and its clients. Engagement in work leads to a "Pride in performance" and better results and sense of growth. This leads to greater attachment and loyalty to the organization.

Cultivating such a culture where end users feel safe, comfortable and valued results in better social connections, empathy to one another, collaboration, and encouragement at the work place.

This Chapter takes a DEEP DIVE into the very Process of Designing Work spaces that creates a Positive Work Culture & Work space Vibe, thru a meticulous sequence of 30 Steps, carved out of a 30-year work experience as an architect!

While the steps may overlap or in some cases be irrelevant, the focus is to make 30 dots on the journey of Designing Positive Work spaces and join them with an invisible cord! I would like to call these 30 pearls of Wisdom that fast forward younger architects to more appropriate ways of designing work spaces!

The legacy of Designing Good Work spaces with Positive Attributes needs to be forwarded to the Next generations most selflessly! Here are the Five Key Attributes to Designing Positively to enable Positive results; each Attribute has Checklists that add up to 30 meaningful points on the bucket list to success!

5.1: Understand

Nowadays People Just hear, they do not Listen! The Key to doing well is to Understand, Listen and Consolidate! It is not the Hearing that improves life, it is the Listening! "Listening is not a skill, it's a discipline" says Dr Peter Drucker, Author and Management Guru!

"When you talk, you are only repeating what you already know! But if you listen, you may learn something new"

The Dalai Lama

Here's what we feel makes the difference:

Step 1: Understand Client Requirements

"Most people do not listen with the intent to understand, they listen with the intent to Reply!" Stephen Covey, Author of 7 habits for Highly Effective people.

Perhaps the Simplest of tasks is the Starting Point for Designing Well! In a world that is increasingly noisy and cacophonic, we need to be Good Listeners, first and foremost! Sounds easy but often this is the first point of failure!

Your client is the key to this! He needs to be heard and his every word is a clue to what he seeks from you! We often fail to take notes and record key words and phrases that attempt to explain an idea that may be the key to something special!

A Quote by Dean Jackson sums it up well: "Listening is an Art that requires Attention Over Talent, Spirit over Ego and Others Over Self!" It is thus imperative that this task be led by the senior most (rather than be delegated to the junior most of people)!

Client briefing and understanding is as important a first step as ever and needs to be attended to with diligence and dedication. It's even more paramount in a Post pandemic World! It's akin to a doctor seeking from the patient all that ails him; the remedy lies in the ailment!

Recommendations:

- Unless properly captured in a purposeful and intent-full RFP, never trust a hand me down document of needs! The Client brief needs to be recorded and referred thru the life cycle of a project; it may start somewhere and end somewhere else, but it's a journey whose origin needs to be marked!
- Speak to the Right Persons: Often it's the HR / FM who briefs re the project, but its CEO or MD who gives the valuable insights and over rides the others; don't miss them! You do not want two diverse briefs later on!
- Share a Format of requirements that helps extract the right information is as easy a manner possible, probably on a Google form format.
- The Work Space "Story" Lies in the "brief"!
- And the "brief" ... must inspire the "Story"!
- In Brief... it's all about the Questions you ask and the answers you take!

Step 2: Understand the TWINS: Brand Identity & Aspirations

Offices are mostly about Brands. Every office has a unique name, website and Vision / Mission Statement, invariably that defines the brand identity of the Organisation you are working for!

But Post Pandemic, there is even greater need for the Brand to be expressed! The Brand serves as a magnet that attracts people to one central belief and office vision!

The Brand identity informs you of the clients work culture and the ethos of the company! It informs the history and the Story of the Client over the many years of existence. Stories amount to legacy! People love to hear about legacy! The Design's first cues come from here!

Brand Identity is often just a Manual that mostly talks about the Do's and Don'ts! Brand identity is a lot more than just accepted fonts, styles and proportions of signage! Brand Identity is about the kind of workplace and the way it needs to be. Aspirations, on the other hand, are the current wishes & desires of the current work space occupiers.

They are like twin brothers, often at ease with each other and often at odds! Don't let this confuse and contradict! Let it enrichen! One is Older and One is Younger!

Brand identity needs to be viewed as the origin and sequence of a journey an organisation has gone thru; aspirations are more current and contextual to the local people you are designing for! Levi's may have a brand identity dating back to 1853, but the Aspirations for an India office may be different that for an American office!

So, while Brand identity is about the past & convey Legacy, Aspirations are more in the present & convey Desires!

The Brand identity needs to be researched; the Aspirations need to be interviewed. One tells "Who we are, where we came from and what we do to other people's lives"; the other is more self-focussed: "what we want and how we want!"

Recommendations:

The Following Questions need to be asked to seek out Aspirations:

- What's your Budget? Client Budget is a very important part of the Aspirational talk, as it entails clues for what the office aspires to be!
- What's the Age group of the End users? What's the typical educational back ground of the end users?
- What difference thru local context or influence do you want in your new office over and above what the brand identity prescribes?

Step 3: Understand the Site Attributes & Challenges

The Last Speaking & Listening to… is with your site! Unbelievable, but every site has its own story! Listening to the site and looking for cues is the secret for discovering stories that may lie therein! This is particularly true in heritage buildings and places.

Newer Buildings also Tell Stories of How the sun moves, what quality of light comes in, which direction has better views and where and how plumbing and electrical shafts provide connectivity!

"Context is King" is the principle in every good architectural design office! Jumping onto design without understanding the site is a crime! It's like skipping the medical history of the patient and prescribing without a contextual check. Not safe.

In a Post pandemic World, the need for understanding how safe a building is for safe physical entry and egress, washroom capacities and open spaces etc, are aspects to look out for sure!

Every site comes with its own unique challenges that affect design; these need to assessed:

a. Neighbourhood Context
b. Guest Entrance & Emergency Exit clarity
c. Service Elevator and entry Possibilities
d. Site Dimensions and heights
e. Sun Path, Good Views and Adjacencies check
f. Sanitary & Electrical (Esp LV) shafts
g. Status of above and below floors from Insulation point of view
h. Any Historical Elements or attributes of site
i. Quality of External Glazing & Noise and other sources that may be of concern to the site (Like a Railway station, market, or transport hub close by)
j. Any inherited defects (structural, seepage, vandalised windows etc) that need attention before takeover.

Recommendations:

It is highly recommended to invest in Matterport cameras and / or Open space 3D cameras that allow the recordings of the space to the last detail, rather than more traditional modes of measurement.

Step 4: Gap identification & Ideation

As Management guru Dr Peter Drucker says: "The Most Important thing in communication is hearing what isn't said!" Its important to pick up the signals and read between the lines as well! The experienced manage this!

We call this GAP ANALYSIS. What it means is to fill in the blanks between what is asked and what is needed. Many Times, clients rightly expect the Work space designers to understand their industry and requirements and leave it up to them to insert the missing links in the Jigsaw Puzzle.

With the pandemic, the puzzle has only become more intricate, with greater need for understanding what exactly are the priorities for your clients post pandemic office!

There are many examples of this:

A BPO project may not specify the need for Lockers and Turnstiles, but that needs to be understood. A Knowledge processing firm / Consulting office may not mention the need for Individual Partner cabins, but that needs to be sought. A merchandising / garment Firm may not mention the need for Colour Box rooms that need to be assumed. And often even basic aspects like Server rooms, UPS rooms, Electrical Rooms, medical Rooms, Record rooms, Storage Areas, garbage Rooms etc get missed in the brief.

This is where Time saver standards and experience kicks in!

Recommendations:

Typical "Fill in the Gaps" in Modern day offices could be:

- What sort of Storage is needed? (record rooms, Compactors, On Floor Storages, Pantry Stores, Garbage Rooms etc)
- What sort of Infrastructural Support rooms are needed? (Server rooms, Hubs rooms, UPS Rooms, Battery Rooms, Electrical Rooms, pantries, Hold Areas, etc)
- What sort of Work space Welfare amenities are needed? (Mothers Room? Creche? Medical / Sick Room, Quarantine Room, Meditation Room, Nap Room, Prayer Room Etc, Gym / Yoga Room etc?
- What Sort of Recruitment Spaces are needed? (Wating / Holding areas, Interview rooms, etc)
- What Sort of Break Out Spaces & Activity Zones would be used?

5.2: Plan (everything to perfection)

"Plans are nothing, Planning is everything" This quote by Dwight D Eisenhower best describes why an architect is needed and why he needs to be on top of his game to make for Positive work spaces, as also any design.

Its been observed how people love to talk and ideate but when the same things are translated on a plan, its something else. The process of transforming a vision or a dream into a possible reality is the heart of what Good Design is all about!

The Benjamin Franklin Quote: "By Failing to Plan, You are planning to fail" cannot be more apt for the work space domain! The Crux of the Whole Job is to Design a Plan that works and excites its end users! There are Many Aspects of Planning that go into Work space Design that make a world of difference:

Step 5: Focus on The Appropriate Theme

The First & Foremost Aspect of an office is to decide its Theme!

Theme or Concept is really the "Visual Character / Conception" for the space! It defines the thematic ideology of the space and gives focus to the kind of spaces and experiences wanted. Theme tells the Story, and the story MUST be clear!

Theme is what will bring people back to the office in a post pandemic world! Why would people come to a drab office? What would be the reason for them to leave the comfort and safety of their homes to come to work, unless the office had a certain vibe thru a super theme!

Décor Aid Magazine has written a wonderful description for themes, into fourteen categories including what follows (Decoraid, 2019). Extracted here are relevant 10 Themes that apply to Work spaces:

PERIOD THEMES:

Theme 1: Traditional

The traditional style offers a combination of comfortable furniture, classic designs and casual décor. It is a term that includes several design elements, including warm colors and symmetrical lines. The furniture is plush and soft, and many of the pieces are sold as sets. Traditional décor is an expansive category that includes a wide range of decorating styles from French country to neoclassical. Think classic furnishings, elegant wallpaper, beautiful curtains, antique accents, patterned or textured rugs, statement lighting, and last but not least, thoughtful color schemes.

Theme 2: Rustic Country Style

Country style has a typically warm décor, with a significant presence of wood. It is harmonious and adapts to any type of environment where it creates a rustic atmosphere. The top coats are wood coloured or painted in pastel tones. Taking inspiration from the outdoors, rustic theme is based on natural weathered finishes, raw wood, stone, and leather. The Japanese Wabi Sabi is a development on this theme!

Theme 3: Art Deco

Art Deco is a popular design style of the 1920s and '30s characterized especially by sleek geometric or stylized forms and by the use of man-made materials. If your taste veers towards the ornate and jewel-like, this 1920's design style throwback might just be your best option. Art deco interior design instantly evokes opulence; elegant, glamorous and sleek, this style was popularized as the epitome of chic in the 1920's.

Theme 4: International Style

Mid-century modern is the quintessential timeless decor. Also known as an "International Style", Mid-century modern design rose to popularity during the 1930s and 40s but never quite went out of style. ... Defined by organic shapes, minimal decor, and a focus on functionality, this style of interior design is undeniably timeless and relatively simple to emulate at home

Bauhaus architects and designers who migrated to America as a result of economic changes in Germany after the second World War started the design movement known as Mid-Century Modern. It's characterized by simplicity and functionality.

Simply Put it is the Minimalism of the 1930s to 1960s!

MODERN THEMES:

Theme 5: Minimalist

Minimalist Style of design, originating in the 1960's, is one which is devoid of clutter and only presents what is basically needed in the décor; it places high premium "on what goes in" into an otherwise stark, plane and clutter free work environment! Some people may call it "cold", some "a No Decoration" style and others may call is "Clean Elegance"! The **style** of **minimalism** is a design approach that is characterized by austerity in decoration. It is mainly achieved through the use of functional furniture and interior objects, geometric shapes and a combination of usually not more than two basic colors.

Theme 6: Contemporary

The Contemporary style belongs to the moment. Fundamentally, a **contemporary style** of decorating is defined by simplicity, subtle sophistication, deliberate use of texture, and clean lines. Interiors tend to showcase space rather than things. ... By focusing on color, space, and shape, **contemporary** interiors are sleek and fresh.

Theme 7: Industrial

Industrial style or industrial chic refers to an aesthetic trend in interior design that takes clues from old factories and industrial spaces that in recent years have been converted to lofts and other living spaces. ... Industrial style can also be seen in the use of unexpected materials used in building. Industrial style decor comprises of stripped back architectural details including the use of bare bricks, concrete, rusted metal, wood, as also salvaged, recycled materials. Industrial style furnishings are usually hardwearing and often obtained from reclaimed yards.

Theme 8: Eclectic

Eclectic style encompasses a variety of periods and styles and is brought together through the use of color, texture, shape and finish. ... Colors: The palette can vary, but it's best to stick with a few neutrals to help tie all the elements together.

In contemporary society, styles that draw from many different cultural and historical styles are loosely described as "eclectic" though references to eclectic architecture within literature and media are usually about buildings constructed within the eclectic movement of the late 19th-early 20th century period.

Similar to bohemian décor but with a decidedly grown-up allure, eclectic interior design is all about high-energy, spell binding finds and furnishings. Think bold color palettes, textures, and patterns brought together to create a rich mix with utility and focal points in mind. While that may sound like bohemian, there is a key difference between the two. Bohemian throws out all the rules, favoring personal taste above design principles. Eclectic, on the other hand, bends but doesn't break the principles of design. It relies on elements such as balance, rhythm, and proportion and scale.

Theme 9: Asian ZEN

In Asian Zen décor, clean lines feature heavily. Squares, rectangles, and circles are prevalent throughout these designs – oozing simplicity, they are immediately recognizable, allowing your mind to focus elsewhere, without having to consider intricate shapes and designs. Association with natural Light & Nature is strong!

Each Theme articulates an approach / character that then defines the treatment to the following design Approaches!

Theme 10: Futuristic Style

Futuristic design is mainly characterized by its strong chromaticism, long dynamic lines, suggesting motion, urgency, and lyricism. Asymmetry is one of the prominent key features. It comes in walls, and corners in the form of angled cutaways. Thoughtful design in the style of Futurism – it is practical, bright, beautiful and unusual ambience. This style is selected by dynamic, self-confident people who look boldly into the future.

The Clarity of Style and the Appropriateness of its utilisation makes all the difference to the projects Language!

Step 6: Design for Legible Circulation

Theme done... The First strokes of a pencil on paper or a mouse on a screen, depending on which generation you belong to, are invariably concerned with Movement! How do you enter a site and what are the rational Movement patterns!

Why is this even more important in a Post Covid Work place? Well, in an increasingly "physical distanced new normal" there needs to be clarity in the way one moves around the work place! Greater the legibility, better the sense of Wellbeing!

There are two types of Movement: vertical Movement across floors of Buildings and Horizontal Movement across the floor plates; both need to be integrated to ensure a seamless movement!

Components of Circulation

To simplify further, architects typically divide their thinking according to different types of circulation, which overlay with one another and the overall planning. The type and extent of these divisions will be project dependant, but might include:

- **direction of movement:** *horizontal or vertical;*
- **type of use:** *public or private, front of house or back of house;*
- **frequency of use:** *common or emergency; and*
- **time of use:** *morning, day, evening, continuous.*

Each of these types of circulation will require different architectural consideration. The movement

might be fast or slow, mechanical or manual, undertaken in the dark or fully lit, crowded or individual. The pathways might be leisurely and winding, or narrow and direct.

Of these types of circulation, **direction** and **use** are often critical to a building layout

(Architectural Concepts: Circulation, 2020)

Movement (better referred formally as Circulation) is the essence of the plan and defines how people enter and exit the site safely and legibly! Often the movement can be categorised into three broad approaches:

a. The Grid City Approach, as in any structured neighbourhood
b. The Organic Growth or meandering Pattern of Movement
c. The Grand Gesture that Makes the Circulation the key for the Design!

Different kinds of offices have different space indexes and demands on CRE that allow application of one or the other. The Grid City Approach is by far the most appropriate and safe approach that maximises floor efficiencies and allows scalability.

The Organic Growth or the Meandering Path is used to break linearity or monotony in a definite manner that appears deconstructed/ fluidic seemingly allows relating to new age modern Building Container profiles that themselves break geometries.

The Grand Gesture Approach, as I would like to call it, allows for a Circular or Amoebic path within a rectangular confine or a rectilinear approach within a Circular Building floor plate; its more a case of opposites that make the movement a grand gesture in itself!

Recommendations:

Whatever be the approach, the basics of movement entail

- A safe and legible circulation between Point A to B; this should never be lost!
- No dead ends or cul-de-sacs should be encouraged as these become dump yards eventually
- Suitable integration with vertical means of access and egress (both elevators and staircases)
- Clear passages as mandated by National Building Codes (1500 mm or 1800 mm in some cases)
- Clarity of primary and secondary (and sometimes tertiary) movement routes.
- Separate and defined access (for larger floor plates) for Guest and for Service movement.

Step 7: Focus on Massing & Volumes

Work Space Designing: It's Like a City Planning exercise! The Roads and infrastructure are the first to be laid out in a new city after which the building typologies are located strategically! In a similar manner, large plate office designing entails massing and Volumetrics, post Circulation.

Most Architects follow the "Neighbourhood Approach" to planning, wherein zones of self-sustaining blocks of CRE exist in different wings / part of an office and are well connected thru a well laid circulation system.

Massing simply means defining on the plan what constitutes contained spaces and what constitutes open Spaces. Modern day offices tend to work enclosed spaces more around the core and open out towards the views and glazing for the open spaces.

Volumetrics is an understanding of which available areas could be double height, if possible, to manage a sense of drama thru volume! Mostly spaces that work well with volume are receptions, auditoriums, arenas and dual level cafes! Connecting stairs between floors heightens the drama of volume and makes for better vertical relations.

The following factors affect the planning of Massing & Volumetrics:

    a. Clarity between Private V/s Public Spaces
    b. Clarity between Formal V/s Informal spaces
    c. Clarity between Naturally lit v/s Mechanically lit spaces
    d. Clarity between Work spaces v/s Collaboration Spaces

Judicial use of space leads to better site attribute utilisation which is the core of Design! This is more important in a post Covid scenario as Work spaces would be of smaller footprints and would need to use space more meaningfully!

Recommendations:

Certain learnings and Practices over the years:

- Demarcation between Public Space and Private Space are key decisions for most organisations that need to be discussed with the end users.
- Formal and Informal spaces do not work in close proximities and need some sort of enclosed space barriers between the two to work positively!
- Most cabins need to back onto Building & Service cores and not be set against windows. Windows are for all, not the privileged few in the new world order!
- Dark areas like Conference rooms and Training rooms Can be internal as it makes no sense to down black out blinds for large projections.
- Cafes, Training Rooms and recreation can combine to create Townhalls
- Key areas that must have direct sunshine to energise: Cafes, Break Out areas, Ideation spaces, Stepped arenas etc where people would normally flock to!

Step 8: Sort Out Logical Wet Zoning

"If it does not work, it does not work"! Whoever said this, was referring to Plumbing and Sanitation most likely! The Secret of sensible planning lies in the need to plan once and never have

to redo anything again! Planning of washrooms and Pantries is UP on the List of Must Dos... once and for all!

With increased focus on Sanitation and hygiene, it should be no secret, that planning for Wet zoning of Pantries and Wash rooms should be a TOP priority.

In a multi tenanted floor plate building, it is the shortest plumbing and drainage that decides logical placement of washrooms, pantries, bain-maries and indeed break out areas with dispensers. Same is the case of AHU rooms that may need to be added on the floor plates, if not already provisioned by the builder.

Getting the planning right is the first and foremost concern of any FM and is imperative to the success of a design in the long run, way after an architect and the contractors leave a site and hand over to the real estate team.

Recommendations:

Washrooms need to follow Codal provisions depending upon Planned densities; this calculation is fundamental to Positive Work space Designing, wherein the Quality, Optimised Quantity and Design décor of a washroom defines the acceptability of a work space! Washrooms set the bench mark and standards of an office, just like they do in the hospitality domain.

Pantries (both wet and dry) may be planned a little off the core, but greater proximity to wet cores helps simplifying the plumbing and minimising the servicing in later years.

Step 9: Design Social Spaces

Much has been written, in recent times, re the ideation of Work spaces in post pandemic times, with new age expectations of Hybrid work scenarios emerging! Collaboration can happen Virtually, as has been proven during the lock downs, the world over! But ask any work space member if he prefers Virtual or Actual Physical Collaboration! Given that we are Social Animals, the answer is not a surprise.

Social spaces are the heart of the Future Post pandemic work-space for sure; its where work culture emerges, attitudes form, ideation happens and collaboration succeeds! In actuality, this is why Offices are still relevant in a post pandemic Virtual world, as the quality of WE Time is unmatched, in person! There are three kinds of levels of Social Spaces:

    a. Large Group Social Spaces: Like Stepped Arenas, Scrum wall gatherings, High Counters, Media scape zones etc. Often cafes are also included in these zones during non-lunch hours!

    b. Small Team Social Spaces: Booth Seating, High Counters, Break Out Lounge seating,

    c. Individual Social Spaces: Like tele-pods, Quiet Rooms, Focus Booths, and meditation spaces.

New Age offices encourage greater socialisation, both of the planned and unplanned type. The idea is creating an office that disrupts normal usage and

stimulates exploration, interaction and chance encounters! Higher the Collision, Higher the Engagement and so higher the Productivity!

This is the single reason why Co-Work spaces have flourished in the last decade! Jennifer Magnolfi, (Ben Waber, 2014) discovered that people had chosen them because they believed that their performance would improve more rapidly in such spaces than in an office building or at home. A *Deskmag* survey of more than 1,500 co-workers in 52 countries supported her findings:

- 75% reported an increase in productivity since joining their space
- 80% reported an increase in the size of their business network
- 92% reported an increase in the size of their social circle
- 86% reported a decrease in their sense of isolation
- 83% reported that they trusted others in their coworking space

Recommendations:

The Best Social Spaces are those that allow for socialising and do not infringe or disturb quiet work areas; so, the planning of these spaces needs to be done sensibly.

These need to be co-located strategically and create intentional people Collisions that stimulate social interactions and engagement! Chance encounters and interactions between knowledge workers improves performance.

Social Spaces need their fair share of natural views and sunlight with preferable step out balconies or verandas.

Coffee Bars and Vending Machines are also becoming hot spots for social zones and are a welcome addition upfront, near receptions, in co-working areas, as they give a warmer and inviting feel. These need to be planned like magnets that make people galvanise towards them and connect!

Step 10: Create FUN SPACES: Café, Break Outs & Recreation Spaces

There are proven reasons why Breaks at Work are so important for Positivity and productivity at the Work place! This is particularly true as people come back to offices after many months of Full WFH where interruptions and distractions form the new normal! To expect them to get back to hushed office working styles is wishing for what's not going to happen!

Three reasons why Breaks are good at work (Seiter, 2014):

    a. Breaks keep us from losing focus and getting bored
    b. Breaks help us retain information and make connections
    c. Breaks help us re-evaluate our Goals

Even the Harvard Business Review has written *"A 2011 study published in Cognition highlights another upside to sporadic breaks that we rarely consider: goal reactivation. When you work on a task continuously, it's easy to lose focus and get lost in the weeds. In contrast, following a brief intermission, picking up where you left off forces you to take a few seconds to think globally about what you're ultimately trying to achieve. It's a practice that encourages us to stay mindful of our objectives, and, as the authors of the study report, reliably contributes to better performance."* (Friedman, 2014)

When employees take micro breaks, they get the opportunity to recharge and refocus. This way, they can function more efficiently throughout the workday. Standing up from their desks also promote better blood circulation and is better for their overall health. (Seiter, 2014)

Office coffee breaks are also venues for employees to socialise and create positive relationships with one another. Chats over a cup of good coffee is the perfect opportunity to loosen up and know one another better.

But in Many offices Coffee takes the blame... One study even supported this by revealing that Britons waste an average of 18 hours a year to get a cup of coffee from the local shop. Even if a company only has 10 employees, the 180 hours lost is already equal to more than twenty 8-hour days of work lost in a year. For much larger companies, this number will obviously go up. (Sharpe, Coffee: A Workplace Saviour or productivity Killer, 2019)

It has been scientifically proven that coffee can increase energy levels and make people feel less tired. Coffee breaks can help foster positive employee relationships

Employees, working non-stop, may seem like best-case scenario to increase company productivity, however, according to science, this may actually do more harm than good. When employees work continuously for long periods, they tend to slow down and they become more prone to mistakes. This also takes a toll on their physical form causing neck and back strains.

Recommendations:

- It is established that Coffee is a fundamental part of corporate culture. So, finding ways to maximise its benefits is a good way to increase productivity in the workplace.
- Locate Coffee stations in Break Out areas across the Work floor, to minimise time lost, in reaching out for the hot beverage.
- Good offices MUST invest in GOOD Coffee machines so that employees do not need to go out to get their preferred beverage, ever so often!
- Free Coffee & Tea is considered one of the Biggest Employee perks and reasons people love their offices! And it's all about Happy & Satisfied Employees, isn't it?

- Allow Flexible seating Opportunities that allow people to pull up and re configure groups, rather than fixed seats.
- Allow various Typologies of seats that allow different postures than the normal office chair: high counter sit stand option is good, as also, a sunk in relaxed couch or a backless peg stool.
- Acoustics is important at these break out areas; so, locate them sensibly.
- Sunlight, views and greenery make for great settings for Break out areas and cafes.
- Combining these spaces with recreation (pool, snooker, foosball, table tennis and board games / X Box: depending on user age groups) are a great idea.
- Cafes and recreation areas could be multi-purpose spaces that could combine to create large spaces for Town Halls.
- Colour and Vibrancy are key Must haves for the Cafes, break outs and recreation zones which could be incorporated thru: large video walls, stunning wall graphic vinyl, Plants & Biophilic touches, concept flooring and wall claddings etc!
- Coffee bars and Sports Bars: Way to go!

Step 11: Ensure Support Spaces:

"A Goal keeper is not remembered for the Goal saved, as much as he is remembered for the goals, he lets past!" In a similar way, the Support Spaces, in an office, are the Quiet spaces that remain in

shadow, but are essential to the very survival and functioning of the office! They are the engine rooms of the Ship that need to operate quietly and seamlessly for a smooth ride!

Post Pandemic, there would be newer support spaces needed in Work space environments such as medical rooms, isolation chambers, prayer rooms etc. What was once thought peripheral or "maybe" would now be central and "Must have"!

Support Spaces are of a few relevant kinds in work spaces:

    a. IT & Infrastructure spaces: Server rooms, Hub Rooms, Electrical, UPS and battery Rooms
    b. Pantry Support Services: Holding Areas, preparation areas, Serveries, BOH areas, refrigerated areas and garbage rooms.
    c. Storage Spaces: Like Compactors, Record Rooms, Vaults and Cash rooms
    d. End User Support Areas: Prayer rooms, Nap rooms, Locker rooms, etc.

Recommendations:

The Support areas need to be planned centrally to floor plates for ease of access by all or on a neighbourhood basis depending upon floor plate configurations

The Support spaces are best planned to clean up edges of the core and create outer spaces that gel and flow ell with the guest zones.

Support spaces are as important and vital to work spaces, as are "Supporting Roles" to any Awards night for the movies! They are the silent heroes of the work space!

Step 12: Design a Variety of Zones

The new Post Covid Work space landscape has changed; its primary job is to welcome back people who have been used to a "ME" Existence to a "WE" reality thru an intricate web of multiple spatial configurations.

As all Humans are not the same, so also, should all work space offerings not be the same! Variety is the spice of life and things are no different in the emerging new age Work space landscape.

The Key Types of Spaces in the emerging Work space are:

a. **The Social Zone Spaces**: These are Mostly **WE** spaces, where people meet & greet, laugh and play, re-charge & re-energise., such as: Receptions, Cafes, Break Out Areas, Recreations Spaces, Collaboration Areas.

b. **The Work Zone Spaces**: These can be for **ME** Spaces (Focus work areas) such as Work-stations, Cubicles, Cabins and Focus rooms or **WE** spaces (Group or Team Work Spaces) such as Meeting rooms, Conference Rooms, Booth seats, Training rooms, Stepped Arenas, Auditoriums etc.

c. **Support Zone Spaces**: These are **Restricted Use** spaces like UPS rooms, Electrical rooms, Server rooms, AHU Rooms, Store Rooms, Record Rooms, Creches, Mothers Rooms etc or **Common Use** Spaces such as Washrooms, Nap rooms, Medical Rooms, Prayer Rooms, Change Rooms etc.

What is good to know is that All three types of Spaces can be Formal or Informal: You could work from a Work station or a collaboration touch point; you could Meet in a meeting room of a Casual Booth Seat!

With the emergence of the Laptop and increased Mobility of the other handheld devices, tabs etc, the new breed of work space occupants see no need to be chained to one type of Zone; The very possibility of switching between zones is what the new office landscape is all about: Choice.

Agile and Activity based work stations entail a wide variety of work type configurations. Typically, most Agile offices would allow for 80% conventional work stations (pre pandemic) and now have settled for 40-50% (post pandemic). The remaining would float around what is called "Choice seats" thru multiple collaborative space offerings!

Even in offices that are not agile or Activity based, there is need to question "why a one shoe fits all" policy must not be questioned! More and More attention is now being paid to VARIETY!

The key thought behind this need for variety and reduction in formal seating is the low probability of 100% attendance every day, especially post pandemic. Why then should real estate be wasted only one isolated working that can very well happen at home?

An Interesting paper (Wernick & Morris, 2020) written recently talks about the new workplace having more diversity and choice in places where employees can work than ever before, moving away from the one-size-fits-all office for good. One of the most common complaints about the open office is distraction. It's no surprise this is a significant challenge when workers are expected to collaborate and concentrate in one homogenous space.

The paper talks about "The New Workplace Kit of Parts" addressing this by providing distinct spaces for collaboration and concentration, with employees being empowered to choose where they want to work based on the task at hand. The idea is that employees will be more productive when they have the right spaces for the work they need to accomplish.

Recommendations:

- List down the Types of work / activities done by an organisation and then try and cater to those diverse types.
- Ensure the variety of furniture also promotes different seating / standing postures for best health benefits; Remember the saying: "Sitting is the new Smoking!"
- Ensure Different Typologies have different spatial settings as well to allow for them to be in Quiet Work Zones, where needed, and in Social / Collab Zones, where needed.

Step 13: Check on Space Optimisation & Balance Review

You and your employees will spend at least 40 hours per week (and about 2,000 hours per year!) in the office. Well, maybe it reduces to half and half for WFO and WFH, post pandemic. But the fact remains that the work space needs to be increasingly optimised and utilised.

How you organize the space between those four walls can affect not just aesthetic appeal but also comfort and how much work gets done. (Carter, 2020)

Office Space Optimization Software, that helps optimising Room and resource management, is now available for end users.

However, when it comes to Design, it's important to imagine a plan to use existing space well without cramping up or affecting a balance of open and covered space. Optimisation & Balance Check of a plan is a sign off by a work space specialist who would look into:

   a. If the plan has clarity of thought and uses space uniformly without some areas being over dense and others sparse.
   b. If the Layout has similarity in dealing in all its sub-parts and does not look disparate to each other (if the space usage is the same)
   c. If nooks and corners and edges are well utilised without having to create dead closed off spaces!

In fact, In addition to "Balance", the other 6 of the 7 interior design principles are: Emphasis| Contrast| Rhythm| Scale and proportion| Harmony and unity| Details. All these help in creating Positive Design Spaces and are often used by experienced architects.

Recommendations:

It is recommended to imagining the office plan like a small city, where there would be streets and blocks, as also, open spaces that are vital to any city! Basically, Workspace plans need to have spaces to stand (& Congregate) as well, not just sit!

Design work spaces, as you would plan cities: there must be streets and nodes and pockets of tranquillity in between; but space must be well used and well distributed.

Step 14: Ensure a Definitive Colour Scheme

Interesting to know that there are 7 Design Elements that need to be considered in Interior Design with Colour being first and foremost! What are the 7 basic elements of design? The seven elements are **line**, **color**, **value**, **shape**, **form**, **space**, and **texture.**

However, this Check List is all about Colour.

There are all types of work spaces and all types of décor! If there is one thing that stands out and becomes memorable for an office for the end user (and the visitor) it's the Colour Scheme!

Whilst Colour schemes are mostly inspired from handed down brand identities, there are occasions where designers come with out of the box solutions that make a difference! What makes some offices have a wow colour scheme that looks mature and balanced? And What makes others look gaudy and over cooked?

While colour is the most discussed subject in design on the planet, there are a few concepts I follow which I would like to share, when it comes to work space colour schemes; for this it's important to understand three types of colours in any office palate:

Base Colour (Dominant Theme Colour): Could be Greys, Beiges, or tones of wood, typically.

Balancing Colour (Support Role Colour): Could be Whites, Greys, wood tones or even blacks

Accent Colour (Hero colour / Pattern): Could be any other Colour from the spectrum: VIBGYOR (Violet, Indigo, Blue, Green, Yellow, Orange or red!) or a print (floral, Animal, geometric, self-patterned etc)

There are no Rules of the Colour Theme Game; just like the colour of the year changes every year, so do perceptions of colour theories. However, some indications for starters would help, as shared here and applied on the mentioned Thematic possibilities earlier:

Period Themes	Base Colour	Balancing Colour	Accent Colour
1. Traditional	All Colours / Patterns	Pastels & Prints	Darker wood tones

2. Rustic Country	Terracotta, earthy browns etc	Off whites, creams	All tones of wood
3. Art deco	Chequered patterns and contrasts	Richer tones, materials or visual textures	Pastels & brass or metals & mirrors
4. International Style	Pastel tones on lighter side & patterns	Restrained tones of terracotta, ochre, racing green etc	Dark polished Woods

Modern Themes	Base Colour	Balancing Colour	Accent Colours
5. Minimalist	Greys / beiges	Whites / Charcoal	Wood Tones
6. Contemporary	Whites / Greys	Whites	Metal / Wood
7. Industrial	Grey cement	Whites / Charcoal	Metal / Wood
8. Eclectic	Anything	Anything	2-3 colours
9. Asian Zen	Neutral or earthy	Whites and beiges and greys	Pastels
10. Futuristic Style	Black or White	Polished and smooth surfaces; no wood	Metallic tones and neon colour changing lights

Recommendations:

- Work Spaces are very context and culture specific! So, Work spaces, despite any theme, needs to have more colour and spice in warmer climates of South East Asian countries & South American countries! All countries, near and around the equator like some chutzpah!

- Whichever the décor, never overcook it! It is important to always seek an eternal flavour; this can be achieved by keeping accent colours to under 33% of the office landscape.
- Colour theme, finally, depends upon the end user typology; a lawyer's office or a Doctor's office may be more European; a Design office or a BPO may be more American / SE Asian.

Step 15: Create Multi-Functional Spaces

One of the Most Powerful words in current Work space terminology is "Choice". There are Enough studies that have shown that Employees who are given Choice are far more engaged and productive than those without this enablement. This is particularly more important for a populace that's coming back to offices post a long duration of WFH, where choice was omnipresent!

This has been the case for the past decade; the table below from a Gensler Work place report in 2013 proves the facts that Choice enables greater innovation, better performance, Job Satisfaction and Workplace Satisfaction, more that anything else. Greater Choice is Empowering and makes for a Mindset that is positive and action oriented and liberating.

Modern Work places have understood this and now CHOICE has led to FLEXIBILITY! This entails the potential of being able

to assemble and re assemble into a variety of work configurations based on the nature of activity!

For example, a meeting table can be easily resized by attaching or detaching modular components of the table. These modular components can be easily moved around because they are on wheels. Desks and workstations can also be moved around easily because they are on wheels. This allows the dynamic creation of new teams and boosts collaboration between workers for short-term and long-term tasks.

Typical Areas that benefit from this are Activity areas that reconfigure from "Training room mode" to "Activity Mode / Banquet Mode" to "Conference table Mode" to "Perimeter facing mode"! Such Multi-Functional Spaces are Gold dust in an office and save lots of OPEX by saving on leasing such spaces extraneously!

Increasingly, cafes are also being counted in this category; when combined with Training rooms, they create wonderful opportunities for Town Halls and Joint Sessions with connected AV equipment helping the purpose.

An interesting post (Wernick & Morris, 2020) mentions that *"The energy of the workplace should be designed with intention and purpose. We often call this the acoustic landscape of the office as it maps the full spectrum of spaces from "hot" or active to "cool" or quiet. The "hot" zones support louder, more energetic activities, while the "cool" zones support more focused work. The New Workplace Kit of Parts covers the full energy spectrum with a variety of "hot" spaces, "cool" spaces, and "transition" spaces in between.*

While we believe the new workplace will prioritize collaborative and community space, it must accommodate and promote all styles of work – collective and individual, active and quiet – to enhance employee performance and ultimately improve satisfaction and retention. This promises a more diverse, varied and indeed richer environment."

Recommendations:

The Post pandemic Work spaces are increasingly embracing Choice & Flexibility to the erstwhile territory of Fixed work hall areas! The fixed seats are coming down and more areas are being allocated to Open and Flexible seating! Good Offices are becoming more and More Multi-Functional! More on this later!

Step 16: Plan for Future Growth

Plan for Growth

A critical consideration while making plans for your office layout is "Planning for growth". It is important to plan for the unknown future and decide on how many employees would be added in the next 6-12 months, and how (and where) would they be seated?

Further questions that arise are:

How will this additional foot traffic affect common spaces and facilities?

Will meeting rooms be constantly booked?

Will Washroom Numbers change?

Will support activities like pantries and self-help counters serve the purpose?

Will Café capacities need to change?

Will mandatory Compliances get affected?

Organize your space with the future in mind so you don't have to reorganize and re-furbish out of necessity, too soon! While the occasional office reorganization is normal, let it not come as a rude surprise.

In a post Pandemic world, growth could be positive or negative, as well. Instead of looking at how many more people would join the office, it could also be a case of estimating how many would continue to WFH. So, it's a double-edged sword, post pandemic.

Recommendations:

Always plan for future growth first as a Master Plan; then remove and reduce the occupancy with movement or collaboration spaces. This allows all services from HVAC Capacities to under floor wiring to be planned to optimum capacities from day one! If you fail to plan (for the future), you plan to fail (in the future)!

5.3 Layer

Once plans are made, the job is not done; the ground is set for Layering with many aspects of Completion for the Planning of an Ideal Work space! Its like making a delicious cake and imagining there will be takers for it; if that was the case efforts to icing and adding the bells and whistles would not be an industry in itself!

Simply put the physical arrangement of space needs to be made to work! It needs to be layered with Functionality and décor that builds on the Physical planning and adds other dimensions!

Step 17: Ensure Security & Safety Compliance

Not the most favourite of subjects for any Architect or Interior Designer, but the key for FMs and HR teams is the need for a safe and secure work space environment! 9/11 changed a lot of things forever; the most primary has been the need for enhanced security and safety of the work place! Well, Covid has just ensured that "safety" is now, even more important than security!

There are many levels of Security, depending on the threat which could be external, internal or virtual; some of these are:

a. Screening / Validating entry for Guests and employees is a concern that needs to be rigorous and systematic to ensure no unwarranted tail-gating in large organisations and no lapse in identification at turnstiles and access-controlled doors.

b. Screening / validation of separate elevators for guests as well as service entry is another major concern area.

c. Security against natural calamities like Fire is an equal concern that requires placement of Fire Hydrants and extinguishers appropriately across the floor plates.

d. Accessible and Legible Fire Escapes that are of mandated width as per national Building codes are another aspect to check out on plan.

e. Mandatory passages and fire escape routes, signage and access to staircases and fire elevators and refuge terraces are vital.

f. Cyber security and prevention of hacking thru a system is a subject in itself which needs to be discussed and provisioned for.

g. Concerns for the appropriate materials on floors to enable non slip passage are also considered a security and safety issue.

h. Finally, Covid has forever taught us a plethora of concerns for which an entire covid plan showing distancing, demarcation of circulation and divisioning of work desks (what I call the 3D's).

So how does all this affect the Positive mindset? Well, it's clearly established that Safety is at the intersection of Physical, Mental and Cognitive well-being! Would

you feel safer on a lonely ranch in the wilderness or in a Multi-tiered gated community! The same applies to the work space! The safer we feel in a work space, the more at ease can we be at work!

Recommendations:

Check if the Plans made address these vital safety and security concerns and get a sign off on the same; missing any of these is fatal. It's like the life of a Goal keeper, again: he is remembered not for the goal he has saved, but for the ones he has let past!

Step 18: Plan for Vibrancy & Buzz

It's already been established that the Post Pandemic Workplace will need to work like a magnet to bring people back to the new emerging office! This is where you need the new work-spaces to have a buzz: what we call "Vibrancy"!

How do you plan for Vibrancy? Can you Plan for people to feel invigorated and magnetised into motion! Can the Magic of a work place be created, or is it something that just happens in some places and does not happen in others!

The Dictionary defines *"Vibrant: full of energy and enthusiasm. Spirited, lively, energetic, full of life"*. A vibrant workplace connotes energy, positivity, and growth—characteristics we desire for the environment where we spend the majority of our waking hours. (White, 2017)

Vibrancy is a sense of feeling "connected" at three levels: to each other, to one's work place and most importantly to one's own inner self! There are a lot of behavioural aspects that bring about a sense of Vibrancy such as connectivity and appreciation.

Well Vibrancy cannot be designed; it can be goaded, stimulated and cajoled thru the physical work environment! In all my years of work space design, I have found the following tend to make spaces vibrant and have a sense of palpable energy:

a. **Good Natural Lighting**: Ensure work spaces allow people to use well-lit areas better and areas with positive views in a more meaningful manner; natural light and views are Gold dust that need to be sensitively used and planned; the more it is equitable and available for all, the better the work place vibe would be! The best designed offices are those that focus on this from the very beginning; having said that, offices can also be retro fitted into creating vibe and value.

b. **Focussed ART**: We are wired to respond to Art and Craft in a manner that's so intrinsic to human nature that it would need a psychologist to delve deeper into the human brain to assess why! Art needs to be planned thru placement at planning stages thru strategic walls and corners, bends and turns. Art could be framed, wall graphics or even graffiti!

c. **Colour**: Accented use of Colour can promote a sense of Buzz and Vibe that works wonders! But needs to be used selectively.

d. **Smell of Coffee**: Fortunately, "procaffeination" is supported by science: Studies suggest that consuming **caffeine** can help promote creativity, concentration, and even prevent **workplace** accidents. Plus, **coffee** breaks are linked to better morale and collaboration at work.

e. **Cool Casual Chic**: Elements like Stepped seating, casual bean bags, ceiling suspended swings, Freedom of seating styles, plethora of collab spaces (all mentioned before) add to the Vibrancy of a space!

Recommendations:

Too Much of Art is Too much! Remember a Good work place is NOT a Museum or Art gallery and the right Balance needs to be struck. Infact, too much of anything of the above is too much. It's like sugar, which can be a sweet poison, if spread around too much!

Step 19: Ensure Glocalization thru AV Technology

Amongst the many things that Millennials crave for, one need stands out way above others! Millennials need "Connectivity" of another sort, as well and the ease of it: That with the Outside world.

Thus far, the talk has been how to promote internal connections and social bonds; but the Global citizen today needs to be Glocal, which, as per Wikipedia is defined as: "reflecting or characterized by both local and global considerations." The term "**glocal management**" reflecting the notion of "think globally, act locally" is used in the business strategies of companies, in particular, by Japanese companies, that are expanding overseas."

Good Audio Visual (AV) Technology allows people to connect virtually like never before and this has seen the biggest growth in the Post pandemic Virtual World! Work spaces need to be wired and planned the same way. There is need to facilitate three kinds of activity in a work place seamlessly and effortlessly, formally and informally:

a. Connecting: with colleagues and clients around the world
b. Presenting: to clients and decision makers around the world
c. Browsing: the websites and links around the world

This Digital Transformation needs to be planned for thru better allocation of budgets for AV in an ever expanding, connected and glocalised world! AV is not the domain of only contained spaces and go to rooms, but even needs to be planned "On the Go and with the flow"!

Given the fear of infection, people are avoiding touching things as much as possible. In corporate applications, as well as the education, government, hospitality, entertainment and healthcare sectors, voice-interactive video walls are going to be more indispensable than they ever were.

Application of video walls and Active LED walls of all shapes and sizes, for business visibility and sharing of important information via digital signage is going to become a priority for most businesses in the post-pandemic induced changed world.

Social distancing and COVID-19 have altered the video and audio capturing plans for most industries. Digital displays are increasing in size, shapes, technical advancements and quality to accommodate and engage an increasing number of viewers. Digital signage technology helps connect individuals, boost engagement, enhance immersion, broadcast information, and foster collaboration.

Besides, audio conferencing tools to communicate effectively with large or small groups are also going to empower collaborative spaces with seamless, glitch-free communication.

AV technology has changed the way we communicate and interact, especially in the workplace, where collaboration is the key to productivity and the cornerstone of your company's success. The ability to connect anywhere at any time has employers scrambling to provide their workforce the most advanced AV products on the market. Below are the top three AV trends to undertake before your organization re-designs your new workspace, now and for the future.

1. Get Your Adaptation ON with Flexible Workspaces

Traditional workspaces are the dinosaurs of the corporate world. Today's employees want adaptable, flexible workspaces. With a more digitally enhanced work environment, you can expand your operations and become more efficient. You can move staff meetings to the kitchen. You can stage an impromptu brain-storming session in the lounge. You can listen to your Town Hall on that ultra-comfortable leather couch near the best view in the building! (Netrix, 2019)

Inspiration can come from anywhere! From within the office as well from outside the windows! Just by being more mobile within your office space, you were able to look out the window and get a Brand-new video idea. Suddenly, the video goes viral and you become the star!

Flexibility thru hot desking, remote working, and video collaboration. These can all foster better teamwork.

2. Get AV Tools that Enhance a Collaborative Workspace

For a more collaborative workplace, you'll need the right AV tools. This goes beyond giving your employees the ability to connect anywhere in the world at any time. With the right Audio-Visual Technology package, you can gain the ability to be more productive, more efficient, and more collaborative than ever. Share screens simultaneously. Record your meetings and store them on to the cloud for your teammates. Open a chat group to get some perspective.

The key to enhancing a collaborative workspace is to get software that is accessible to all skill levels and extends across all platforms. You need the ability to share content with your organization. (Netrix, 2019)

3. The IoT ("Internet of Things") Experience is happening

IoT, is about *"extending the power of internet connectivity beyond computers to a whole range of other things, processes, and environments. Those connected, smarter, things are used to gather information, send information, or both".* **Author:** *Calum Mcclelland*

It's important to think about the future of AV technology, especially when the marketplace has seen such a huge explosion of IoT-connected devices in the last few years.

In case you sneezed and missed it, IoT is busy dominating the world and already automating workplace

functions, from temperature and lighting sensors to voice-activated apps that allow you to access documents or book a meeting room or ask about the company's holiday schedule, affecting your entire organization from HR to Upper Management. If voice-activated apps make your personal life easier, imagine what automation and IoT-connected devices can do for your work life.

One thing is certain: There's nothing more powerful than having the most advanced AV products at your disposal in the workplace. (Netrix, 2019)

Recommendations:

- Spread out the AV Layering across the plan, to make it within reach of all, rather than just a privileged few.
- AV facilities need not be contained only but can be in open as well: media-scapes and AV Booths are emerging new trends that foster better connectivity and usage "on the go and with the flow".
- Video walls are a new age must at the reception: Nothing projects and protects the right messaging of a Work space better than upfront!

- Smart screens and interactive displays that allow two-way communication are increasingly more popular than one way interaction.
- Short throw Projectors and Screens are in; conventional long throw projectors that need spaces to be darkened are increasingly being avoided unless needed for specific purposes for large gatherings.

BYOD (*"Bring Your Own Device"*) and enterprise mobility is projected to grow by leaps and bounds. As most of the professionals return to work in a phased manner, BYOD would be rapidly adopted by most companies as their integral workplace policy to avoid physical interaction with the touch interfaces in the rooms.

Whether it is a laptop, mobile or a tablet, employees will have the freedom to use the BYOD device that they like most, in and outside the office to access enterprise data. This will help the collaboration going on without multiplying the chances of a virus spread while saving the company from purchasing or replacing the technology.

Step 20: Provide for Technology Layering

The Post Covid Work space will forever be more tech Enabled. It will be the everlasting change that Covid brought into the work space landscape. Beyond AV, there is a lot more technology that needs to be layered on and provisioned for at the stage of ideation.

> # Technology is what drives and supports businesses today, from apps that enable communications to smart conference tables that allow anyone at a meeting to share their screen with the press of a button.

Here are some tech tools we've come across that will turn your office into a modern digital masterpiece: (unknown, 7 Must-Have Tech Tools for the Modern Office, n.d.)

a. Office automation control system

Buildings are becoming "smart" with automated systems heating, lighting, air conditioning, and so on. Now offices can benefit from the same types of technology. With an office automation system, you can control every aspect of your work environment right from your iPad or mobile device. Some systems even have built-in sensors that can adjust the environment based on the number of people in the office. This allows you to provide the optimum working environment for your employees while also saving you money on energy. A win-win!

b. **Visitor management system**

Digital visitor management systems have become staples of modern digital offices. In work spaces without receptionists, visitor management systems expedite the visitor check-in system, while also reducing the number of interruptions caused by guests and deliveries. In work spaces with someone at the front desk, visitor management systems replace old-fashioned sign-in sheets and enhance security by keeping a record of everyone who goes in and out of the office. It can also help visitors get to the human interaction part of their visitor much faster if the receptionist happens to be on a call, busy with their myriad of other tasks, or away from the desk.

c. **Connected chairs**

Modern office workspaces are all about choice. Many companies outfit their spaces with regular desks, standing desks, couches, and bean bag chairs, so employees can choose where they work at every moment. For maximum productivity, however, your workspace needs to be both comfortable and functional. Well, it hardly gets any more comfortable and functional than this: an office chair that sports an electrical outlet and USB ports. It even has a flip-up privacy panel, so a single work area can provide opportunities for both interaction and privacy, depending on the employee's needs. A couch version is also available.

d. **Treadmill desks**

Standing desks are so last year! Walking is much better for getting those creative juices flowing, and studies link using treadmill desks to improved memory and concentration, attention to detail, and increased productivity. As a bonus, you get some great exercise while being productive.

Recommendations:

Optimizing office space through flexible floor plans and scheduling technology, not only gives employees greater satisfaction and the ability to work the way they prefer, but helps companies increase their employee-to-desk ratio, ultimately reducing their real estate and operational costs and increasing the return on facilities investments. (Carter, 2020)

Offices now need to have Digital Technology Consultants who can advise on the range of new age technologies mentioned, and more (website, 2021):

- **Desk management** (Facilitating: Floor Plan Onboarding; Desk Booking app; desk Social Distancing; People Finder; Way Finder; Analytics, Seat Allocation; Work from Home rostering; Monitor utilisation with sensors; contact tracing)
- **Smart meeting Room Booking** (Onboarding Meeting Rooms; App for booking meeting rooms: Meeting room displays; Sanitisation status and requests; Occupancy Control; Contact Tracing; IOT Integrations; Ambience & Thermal Controls; Seamless check-in)
- **Visitor management System** (Contactless Access; Health Declaration; Temperature recording; detailed Visit Logs)
- **Space Management** (Request for more or less space; Demand Automation; Lease management; Integration with AMS; Move Management; Impact Analysis; AI recommendations)

These are the new age add-ons that make a difference.

Step 21: Check Lighting Lux levels

As per a research paper by Philips Lighting "We spend 80% of our time indoors, and working for over eight hours in poor light can be exhausting.

Recent lighting industry research shows, however, that the right office lighting not only makes the office environment more appealing, it can raise office workers' productivity and bring a range of health and well-being improvements as well as financial benefits.

But different individuals and different tasks require different lighting requirements so one solution is to give people control over the brightness and spectrum of white light in their offices." (Philips, 2015)

Below, Philips has summarized the basic findings that lighting professionals, architects, building designers and business owners need to know.

"Brighter office lighting brings a range of benefits We receive over three quarters of our information through our eyes. Around 50% of our brain is involved in processing that information, and poor lighting makes it a struggle to make sense of what we're seeing".

Offices need to optimise natural lighting and balancing with supported artificial lights. The Uniformity and balance of Light improves the work environment and reduces dark areas; this is a key aspect to creating a positive lit space!

Philips advises that "Using natural light, increasing light levels up to around 1000 lux, and employing cooler light tones can all be beneficial."

Better lighting of around 1000 lux, can actually lead to Better Productivity, Mood enhancement, Job Satisfaction and Organisational Commitment at work.

This is enabling of the following:

a. improved visual clarity & sharpness
b. Increased concentration levels and alertness
c. Greater ease and speed in reading
d. Reduced Eye strain, Fatigue & Headaches

While much lower and warmer light levels:

a. A Hospitality & Wellness feeling
b. An Increased creative vibe
c. An enhanced level of Cooperation

So, while some people find warm lights good for certain types of activities at certain types of timings, others find white lights good for similar reasons. This has led to the notion of personalised Lighting wherein colour temperatures are tuneable to individual preferences. Whilst the technology seems expensive, the productivity it brings to different types of people is amazing.

It is not just the colour temperature of the lighting, but the intensity of it also that can be controlled; there are apps now that can remember your preferences and switch to your likes and dislikes as you move to different zones of the same work space.

While lighting can be adapted and customised, the fact is that different user groups have different preference based on the Type of work they do, the age group and their programmed sense of individual wellbeing.

The Philips research shows that "older people need significantly more light than younger people to see the same detail. And sub-optimal lighting can lead to eye strain, headaches, and other problems that affect productivity." (Philips, 2015)

But Who controls the lights and how feasible is this for everyone to have an app-based control mechanism in a modern work place? This being a problem there is a new technology available: Circadian or Human centric Lighting.

Human centric lighting (defined by Lighting Europe) is a type of lighting that can benefit the biological, emotional, health, or wellbeing of people. This is achieved by dimming the smart light source, most likely an LED, to mimic the levels of sunlight throughout the day.

Timer based Lighting is a further step in the direction of automation that relates to adjusting the temperature and intensity of light across different times of the day to allow for enhance engagement and productivity.

Human Centric Lighting enhances human performance, comfort, health, and well-being by balancing visual, emotional and biological benefits of lighting for humans. It also improves alertness and concentration during learning by providing a better light environment.

A Paper **"Human-centric office lighting 'boosts productivity'"** cites how THE INSTALLATION of 'human-centric' lighting at the Amsterdam office of CBRE has increased productivity by 18 per cent, results of an experiment show. Additionally, work accuracy improved by 12 per cent, 76 per cent of employees reported feeling happier and half felt healthier. (Maloney, 2017)

Decades of research have shown that light has a significant influence on our mood and ability to concentrate – and one of most important aspects of good lighting is timing. Our brain regulates the circadian rhythm of the body based on 'light signals' from our environment. The circadian rhythm controls our energy level, mood and sense of alertness or sleepiness. When our inner clock no longer functions synchronously with the time of the day, we become agitated and our reactions slow down – we are less attentive and it becomes more difficult to concentrate. (Maloney, 2017)

Recommendations:

While there are certain norms to Lighting and Lux level requirements prescribed by the national Building Codes, Lighting can never be generalised. Lighting needs to be planned keeping in mind the following:

- End User Type of Work / Industry
- End user Average Age group
- Dependence on Colour rendition
- Work Hours and needs for Light temperature variation
- Budgets
- Natural Light quality
- Glare Sensitivity

It is well recommended to combine ambient lighting along with task Lighting for a better Work space experience to reduce transition between focussed work and looking up elsewhere.

Lighting is a matter of great research and experience; for the initiated, it is advisable to consult Light manufacturers / Lighting experts / Consultants for best results.

The best Lighting happens when "INTENT" is clear and when INTENT is based on user experience + user Convenience. Ignoring one or the other can lead to an un-fulfilling experience.

Step 22: Design for Acoustic Concerns

The Pandemic made our cities quieter and us humans less used to sounds of the past! If anything, we have been lulled into a quieter world, having worked from homes, in quieter neighborhoods and less populated streets during the lockdowns!

Perhaps the most under estimated aspect is the last, but not the least important segment of Layering: everything to do with the need to control acoustics at the work place for better sense of calmness and control.

The Most Important aspect of Noise is to understand it travels Volumetrically and thus acoustics has to be controlled from three stand-points: Direct Sound, Reflected Sound and Reverberated sound.

Now, you cannot do much about direct sound, other than create administrations norms of allowing them in contained acoustically treated pods, rooms etc and disallow them in open work spaces.

Reflected sound can and needs to be controlled by the architect / work space designer through careful and intelligent materiality for the floors, walls and the ceilings.

Reverberated sound happens only in isolated spaces with mostly amplified sounds; and so gets out of the equation for an architect, unless it's an auditorium / town hall which needs acoustic detailing.

Whatever the nature of sound, excess sound causes disturbance, lower engagement, lower concentration, lower productivity, greater disenchantment, irritation and fatigue. The same work spaces so thoughtfully designed otherwise, tend to start becoming irksome, bothersome and counterproductive, if acoustics is not handled well!

There are many ways to control acoustics in a work place; as per a Blog by a consulting firm Sound Zero, there are 10 ways to better manage acoustics in a work place (Website, n.d.)

1. **Thoughtful Space Allocation of teams** (some teams are typically noisier like Sales & marketing and best be away from say Finance and accounts)
2. **Assigned Meeting Rooms / Quiet** Areas (the work hall may have separate meeting rooms / collab spaces for noisy discussions and / or focus tele-pods and Quiet rooms within the work space itself)
3. **Separate defined area for Break Out & Cafes** (These should be secluded away from Quiet work areas and Focus cabins etc)
4. **Plants** (Unbelievably they also contribute to acoustic Absorption)

5. **Acoustic ceilings / Acoustically Treated ceilings** (These need to be in departments which are typically noisy)
6. **Acoustic treatment for Noisy Rooms** (Like AHU rooms and other areas; containing the sound from within the room where the source is, is the key, along with special treatment to the ducts that enter or emerge from these areas)
7. **Sound absorbing walls & Floors** (As Sound travels volumetrically, its important to have walls, floors and ceilings treated according to acoustic projections)
8. **Linings Under the desks** (As the desks account for almost 40% of the surface, acoustic lining on the under side is a good idea)
9. **Playing Ambient Noise** (Low level ambient sound of a water feature or soft piped music helps drown chaotic un predictable sound that may emerge from chatter)
10. **Feature Partitions** (Acoustic vertical surfaces like perforated screens etc can be a useful addition to the office landscape)

Recommendations:

There is one Quick Fix solution to Acoustic planning for work spaces: Acoustic Treatment needs to be identified with the user group in the following ways:

- Identify and define noisy zones and treat them acoustically at the points of origin thru acoustic materials on all hard surfaces: walls, floors and ceilings.
- Identify Zones where people can go to for noisy discussions such as closed meeting spaces or café or even well located collab areas that are screened off from Quiet Work Areas.

- Mark Quiet work zones in plans in concurrence with the user groups and block them off from noisy areas thru proper planning and massing.
- In addition to Options like Acoustic grid tiles, there are Acoustic baffles, Acoustic clouds, acoustic paints and even acoustic lights now available to treat the work space.
- Push for Carpet instead of hard floors, especially in walk areas, if not entire open work floors; they help reduce sound transmission by approx. 20 decibels or 20- 30%. Next in line are: Cork Flooring, WPC (Wood Plastic Composite), Rubber Floors & Vinyl Floors.
- More Human occupation also increases sound absorption, ironically, as clothes play an important part in absorbing sound.
- The Biggest Acoustic Threat is from Amplified sound that needs to be dealt with in pre-planned closed areas; for the open office the sound emerges maximum from Chatter with workers / phones, Ringing Phones, People walking around, Printer machines and Keyboard clocks.

5.4 EXTRA Concerns

Once the Plans are Layered with the right thoughts and micro-detailing, the focus must move more towards the zone of "Enabling Extra Aspects" that make a difference in the larger frame of things! These are like extra marks achieved in an exam paper that make the difference between doing well and topping! While we dealt with the "MUST DO's", these are the "COULD DO"S" or perhaps the "SHOULD DO"S", as I would like to call them.

Step 23: Grow in a Biophilic Approach

Purposeful designing to reconnect people to nature is the essence of Biophilic design and is increasingly being recognised as the way to humanise work spaces!

Biophilic design is based on the premise that humans intrinsically connect with nature, resulting in better focus, creativity work engagement and sense of well-being. Biophilic design de-stresses and uplifts both Physical, mental and Emotional Health Quotients.

As we navigate through life, changed by COVID-19, the health and wellbeing of those who spend their days in offices are more important than ever. The emotional toll that the pandemic has taken can negatively affect productivity and mental health. Based on a review of more than 50 empirical studies, it has been concluded that an environment devoid of nature can even have a negative effect on health and well-being. Therefore, the use of biophilic design can send out a strong company-wide message that expresses the value of employee health, both physically and mentally. (Wilkins, n.d.)

While Most people think that Biophilic Design entails use of only natural plants, the reality is that anything that transports you towards nature in a sensory manner, is Biophilic. There is no denying that the real effect is thru real means suggested, but even sensual perceptions of the same could do the magic!

The Five Senses relate to the Five Types of Biophilic interventions possible in a Workspace:

a. **Sight**: Sense of Sunshine and brightness may be real or even simulated thru stretched ceilings; as also Visuals and Glimpses of nature thru static imagery or Dynamic means. There is no denying that real green walls and trees make a world of difference, but often hints are also meaningful! Indoor gardens with zen like rocks and water body simulations also make a difference! Biomorphic forms and patterns also create a lasting impression on the mind; sometimes even the shadow or hint of the same thru clever morphing can do the trick.

b. **Smell**: the Actual Fragrance of flowers or the bio mimicry of the same can actually do the same! Fresh mint leaves, tea leaves and the like can inspire the olfactory senses to an illusion of being one with nature.

c. **Touch**: Natural materials like stone, rocks, flowing water, plants elevate the connection of the indoor with the outside. The Worn-out Look of aged materials is what makes "Wabi Sabi" such a rage! Using materials, grains, textures and elements in design that distinctly reflect the natural environment to create an overarching sense of the natural world.

d. **Taste**: Actual Herbal drinks with lemon, fresh mint and other natural flavours in green teas can make a connect in the café, as strong as coffee can.

e. **Hearing**: Cascade water bodies to stand alone recycled water fountains do the job of giving the sensory feel of nature. Sometimes, the sound of nature music can also create the right mood in a space. They also serve as white noise that blanks out the chatter and monotony of an office environment.

The incredible aspect of real greenery is that some species actually help in reducing CO2 levels in a contained work space and improve the Indoor Air Quality index as well by emanating Oxygen during the day! Nature's real air purifiers are being bio-mimicked everywhere, but real is the real deal!

Recommendations:

With health being at the forefront of everyone's agenda, biophilic design in workspaces should be prioritized above anything else. When consulting with clients regarding their wants and needs for the workplace, biophilic design may not always be on their radar, but it should be offered each time.

As soon as you verbalize biophilia's meaning and offer insights on the benefits, people are immediately interested. It is all about how we communicate our plans and provide insights on why it is good for people, makes them much more active in the workplace, and reduces absenteeism. (Wilkins, n.d.)

Step 24: Manage Sustainability Concerns

The Pandemic has exposed the soft underbelly of our pre pandemic time work spaces, and indeed our existence, which were high on consumption and less sustainable in every way! Its has pressed the CTRL + ALT + DEL button quite literally!

A sustainable office design would be able to put together processes and systems that will put a positive turn to how air, water, and the atmosphere are affected. Cut down on the wastage of non-renewable resources and begin to include nature into your design.

Work Design (Weckerling, n.d.) mentions a list of 10 Must Do's that make a lot of sense to bring in the Sustainability Agenda in Work space Design:

1. Go Paperless
2. Ditch Plastic
3. Reduce, Re-use & Re-Cycle
4. Recommend Non-Toxic Cleaning products
5. Limit Heating & Cooling
6. Switch to eco-friendly products & Green certified Materials specification for building the office
7. Embrace Renewable Energy sources to extent possible
8. Create a Green Committee in the office
9. Unplug all electronics at the end of the day (avoid Vampire power losses)
10. Encourage Occupancy based Lighting

Whilst it may not be able to follow all the ten Commandments mentioned, even adhering to a few would be progress with a Capital "P".

Recommendations:

Wherever possible as architects, we can always find materials that are Green pro certified that allow for using products that are more sustainable in their production and disposal.

We may also start adopting a more Circular Design approach that

enables renewed use of materials even after their life cycle, without going to landfill sites.

Step 25: Ensure Inclusivity in Design

For Work spaces to invite back people to their folds, they need to be far more inclusive than ever before!

A Forbes Posting Describes INCLUSION as the following:

"Inclusion can be measured by a sense of belonging, connection and community at work. It's really about how you feel connected to your workplace and the people around you. An organization that has mastered inclusion is one where people feel encouraged to bring their "whole selves" to work. Between voicing diverse points of view and finding a sense of connection to others, this is what makes inclusion real." (hamill, 2019)

Inclusion in the Workplace defines inclusion separately from diversity as "the achievement of a work environment in which all individuals are treated fairly and respectfully, have equal access to opportunities and resources, and can contribute fully to the organization's success."

In the work space Domain, this essentially means equal opportunities for movement, usage of amenities and free circulation with no hindrance for all genders, age groups, income groups and nationalities.

Specific to office design, this means to ensure a "Universal design" better known as "Inclusive design" for people with special needs in particular. Till a few years back, this was not the norm, but now codal provisions world over insist on Inclusivity in design which entails a lot of sensitivity.

By either name, the idea refers to a broad spectrum of ways to produce buildings, products, and environments that are inherently accessible for people with or without disabilities resulting from aging or other conditions, without requiring adaptation or retrofitting. The goal is to provide a workplace that is welcoming, enables everyone to reach the areas needed, and to fully use office equipment and resources.

We've summarized the seven principles that apply not just to facility design, but also to products and environments in general here (Vanderland, n.d.) :

1. *Equitable use:* The design is useful and marketable to people with diverse abilities.
2. *Flexibility in use:* The design accommodates a wide range of individual preferences and abilities.
3. *Simple and intuitive use:* Use of the design is easy to understand, regardless of the user's experience, knowledge, language skills or current concentration level.

4. *Perceptible information*: The design communicates necessary information effectively to the user, regardless of ambient conditions or the user's sensory abilities.
5. *Tolerance for error*: The design minimizes hazards and the adverse consequences of accidental or unintended actions.
6. *Low physical effort*: The design can be used efficiently and comfortably and with a minimum of fatigue.
7. *Size and space for approach and use*: Appropriate size and space is provided for approach, reach, manipulation, and use, regardless of the user's body size, posture or mobility.

Recommendations:

The need for **an all-inclusive policy in design** is a welcome change that has widespread acceptability now; there is need to ensure the following small interventions suggested (Vanderland, n.d.):

- Follow the "closed-fist rule", in which storage units and other equipment has U-shaped handles, push latches, side-hinged doors, and other elements that can be operated with a closed fist — which means that everyone will have access. In the restrooms and break room, provide levers rather than knobs.
- Include ramps instead of — or in addition to — stairs.
- Use different colours for horizontal and vertical surfaces, including changes in elevation, to help those who are vision-impaired, and also reduce the risk of trips and falls.
- Provide lever handles instead of door knobs, or install doors that can be opened with an elbow or even the tip of your nose that make entering and exiting easy for people with limited dexterity — or carrying a laptop and a cup of coffee.

- Adopt adjustable lighting operated by touch panel rather than toggle switches or small knobs.
- Eliminate obstacles in the line of travel in hallways and open-layout spaces.
- Provide blinds or curtains on windows to reduce glare on computer screens.
- Invest in adjustable chairs and desks, with storage in range of reach for all employees, and ergonomic keyboard and computer supports.
- Install multi-sensory safety alarms (auditory; visual), and large-print instructions for emergency and safety equipment.

Step 26: Build in Durability & Serviceability

With the work space increasingly becoming mobile in use, flexible in configuration, Agile and Activity based in functioning, there is need to ensure the new office landscape is designed for durability and Serviceability. With no attachment to any space and all space being "free for all" a "Sense of Ownership" & "Sense of Attachment" does get compromised.

Given the fact that such changes towards workplace flexibility are irreversible, workspaces are becoming more of a "PUBLIC SPACE" than ever before and so need to be designed more durably with ease of servicing.

Some ideas that allow this Greater Durability & Maintenance are:

a. More Durable Full body materials for floors especially, where hard flooring is used (Nylon 6.6 carpet instead of Polypropylene, for example; Engineered floors instead of laminated wooden floors; LVT instead of Vinyl etc)

b. Paints that are more oil based with velvet finish for better maintenance in areas of reach OR a Durable Dado panelling if possible.

c. Use of Materials that are Accessible such as raised floors so that floor conduits / cables are within reach for servicing or upgradation.

d. Wall Vinyl's or 3M Films instead of Painted surfaces withing reach of human touch.

e. Glass instead of solid surfaces that may scratch.

f. Hinged doors instead of Pivoted doors that may need attendance periodically.

g. Aluminium instead of wood to avoid any termite infestation of any sort.

h. Fabrics that are Stain guarded and scotch proofed.

i. Using new age materials like Quartz stone for pantry counters, High Pressure Laminates for Washroom cubicles, and other new approaches are an ever-expanding zone of thought in specifying.

Recommendations:

- It's all about being smart and using "Appropriate Materials"
- Any Area under the foot, specially, needs to be very durable.
- The more we can consider our Work spaces to be designed like good air planes and rail coaches, the better would our response to materiality be.
- Every design decision should be preceded with the question: How will this Material Choice maintain?

- For every service design detailing, the question should be: How easily will this be serviced / accessed few months later!

Step 27: Promote Local Art & Artifacts

Any Work Space needs to have a sense of context!

This has already been written a lot about in current times, at length, and mostly Context has been proclaimed as "KING"!

The Fact is a Multi-national office may have an entire brand playbook available for duplication across offices in different parts of the world, but will always welcome a local touch or influence that gives a "sense of place" and a "sense of pride".

At the end of the day, it's important that an office feels "grounded and rooted" to its reality and location. McDonalds adapts its cuisine and food merchandising according to local tastes within the confines of an overall brand that is recognisable anywhere in the world; the same applies to new age offices that need to present their regional identities.

My favourite saying is: McDonalds uses Sauces and pastes; offices

need to use Regional Aesthetics and tastes!

"If creativity, innovation, and open conversations are elements of an organization's purported culture, the placement of engaging artwork can help substantiate these values and make them visually available." (Smith, n.d.)

Some ways of achieving this are:

a. Displaying art in the workplace increases employee performance, mood, and physical well-being, as well as bolsters interpersonal bonds between the end users.
b. Because our brains hold onto memorable environmental features, art can usefully function as a landmark, helping people traveling through a space to remember where they've been.
c. Amidst many options for addressing branding and company culture in the workplace, art can help communicate key brand messages in a non-verbal way.
d. By this same token, if the art in place illustrates issues of common concern and collective identity — such as environmentally-responsible behaviour etc.
e. Artefacts in 3D add an OOMPH factor and a new age "Selfie Point" for most workers.

Its not just contextuality, its Art that also makes a big difference; recent post (Orr, 2020) cites a study led by Dr. Craig Knight (University of Exeter) who found that people working in an office with art and plants worked 15% more quickly than those working in "lean" environments with nothing more in the space than what was required to complete their tasks. If people were able to arrange the art and plants themselves, in what the researchers called an "empowered" space, their productivity was around 30% higher than those in a very spartan office space.

The Post further states that "Art can also physically benefit a space beyond just filling a blank wall. By enhancing a workspace with art, there is an opportunity to further define and showcase your company brand, culture, and values." aesthetic. After all, as Pablo Picasso said: *Art washes away from the soul the dust of everyday life.*

Recommendations:

Let's promote Art! Art must be encouraged and produced Locally, Vocally to create spaces that have their own character and memorability; that's what good office space design that makes for positivity, is all about! Let's allocate 2% of the budget of a project, for Art work, as used to be the norm, in the past.

Step 28: Soften the Workplace Furnishings

With the increased pandemic induced shift towards "Working from Home", there is also the new return concept of "Homing from Work". What this really means is the need for offices to be less "Stiff Upper Lip" and more informal and millennial friendly for Gen Y & Z.

Resimercial Approach to Design (Residential + Commercial) is the new way of things! What it needs is to deconstruct from a standard palate of materials and adopt a

more residential flavour to commercial settings! This is BIG post the Pandemic when organisations are trying to goad and welcome back people to the workplace, even though on a Roster based schedule!

With people still engaging in the Hybrid work model (2:3) for WFH: WFO, there is greater need to dilute the differences between the two; Offices need to embrace a more home like vocabulary and cater to far more varied palates than before! The Palates could be on softer pastel tones rather than the jarring tones of the past.

Designers have their work cut out to make offices less standard and more theme based; less formal and more relaxed; less monochrome and more varied and vibrant.

Recommendations:

- Minimise Standardisation and maximise variety in soft furnishing and treatments to various parts of the office; an "eclectic" approach is more suitable in some ways.
- Imagine an office to be like a house with Living Rooms, Dining Rooms, Lounges, Guest Rooms, personal Chambers, etc to get the right vibes.
- Ensure different personality types and different work types get taken care of; so large spaces to be avoided and the need is to break down to smaller silos, that are self-sustaining and unique!
- Furniture to be more mixed: Home-like sofas, armchairs, pod seats, and coffee tables.

- Outdoor spaces and spill out areas, as in homes, are more welcome than before.
- Art and Artefacts, as mentioned above, are key players.

Step 29: Plan Out Meaningful Signages

The best Work spaces are those that are most legible and comprehensible; this is the job of Good Signage and Way-finding! Good Signage and way Finding allows for quieter and smoother functioning workspaces!

This is more relevant in lesser populated and drop in offices that will be the new normal of the future! Lesser people with part WFH & part WFO, will mean better and greater reliance to proper signage and legibility of spaces!

Signages in office are of Many types. These need to be designed based on their Location, Impact need and Brand identity. In my opinion, beyond brand signage there are two types of signage: Way-Finding & Safety Signage.

These are normally unknown and ignored.

The Types of Way-Finding Signages:

1. Identification Signages (Showing you have arrived at the right place)
2. Directional Signages (Showing different locations for different sub parts of the Work space)

3. Informational Signages (that assist and inform protocols, timings, registered addresses, statutory information, timings etc)

4. Regulatory Signages (They refer to compliances, Rules & regulations and Access Controls that convey what's allowed and what's not allowed etc)

The Types of Safety Signages are:

1. Prohibition Signs (Shown in reds mostly, indicating Dangerous behaviour, Shut down or evacuation)

2. Warning Signs (In yellow that indicate taking Precautions and being careful)

3. Mandatory Signs (In Blue that ask for wearing specific protective equipment, specific behaviour, action etc)

4. Emergency Signages (In Green indicate emergency escapes, fire evacuation plans, assembly points, routes, equipment, first aid etc)

Recommendations:

Architects need to design signages based on either Brand identity or Compliance & Codal norms. This is an area of adherence more than innovation, mostly. However, newer age thinking is to resort to minimalistic signages that are not over imposing and distracting! The Jury is out on whether signage needs to be minimal or maximal; this depends on the clients sensibilities and how well those can be handled.

5.5 The X Factor

The Last and Final Step in any Checklist is always of Putting it all together! This involves tying up all the loose knots and seeing that by putting the parts together, the whole looks well assembled!

When it is assembled, you need to ask yourself, what is the X factor that typically makes the new office suitable to the end users, so that you can make them feel enthused and excited. If you can answer it, you are there!

The Post Covid Work space needs this X factor to bring back people from the confines of their homes to workspaces that need to be more enticing, inviting and engaging.

Step 30: The USP that Sells

"The future belongs to a different kind of person with a different kind of mind: artists, inventors, storytellers-creative and holistic 'right-brain' thinkers whose abilities mark the fault line between who gets ahead and who doesn't." –Daniel Pink

The USP (Unique Selling Point) of any office is that something special that will be talked about in years to come! It would be that place or feature against which employees would take "selfies" and "groupies"!

It could be a range of things for different work cultures and different contextual settings, such as:

a. It could be that magical Staircase feature that connects the floors of a Multi-tiered work space
b. It could be the Unique Terrace that is landscaped and onto which the office looks onto!
c. It could be the Views of a Wonderful Golf course and the way space is handled looking onto that fabulous view.
d. It could be a Historical element or feature of an Older Building that is meant to give a "context of time" to the setting.
e. It could be a feature wall of pride that showcases the company's history and legacy in a very innovative manner
f. It could be a ceiling that's specially crafted and embellished in some way special with; say waste materials or company produce.
g. It could be a Technology wall in a NOC Room or Gizmo that has been invested in and that holds pride of place and is the first thing you would show a Guest!
h. For many it could be a Work café around which the Whole office could be built?
i. It could be an unusual Flooring treatment that catches attention with everything else being monochromatic, for instance.
j. It could even be the Night Lighting / Transformation of a space into something else than the day time use.
k. Or It could just be a stepped Amphitheatre that takes you back to college and connects vast spaces of double height floors to the mezzanine.

Recommendations:

Don't try too hard to find or create a USP. It is about Serendipity!

If I have learnt one thing: the USP is around the corner, just look for it; don't pre-meditate it. In Cricket parlance: Play the ball on merit, don't pre decide a slog!

To Sum Up:

Post pandemic, the work space demands will only get more intricate, in most projects and for most organisations!

The 30 Points Check List has taken me 30 years of a practice to put together! It Involves five key steps: Understanding, Planning, Layering, Enabling & X Factoring! Together called UPLEX, this involves everything needed for Good Work space Designing.

Even if it is applied, in Part or Parts, it would be better than not applying it to your projects at all!

It's the sequence of going thru this, that's important! Ticking off every box, is not so important!

The 30 Step Road map: Work-spaces Design Checklist: UPLEX

U: Understand

1. Understand Client Requirements
2. Understand the Twins: Brand Identity & Aspirations
3. Understand the Site Attributes & Challenges
4. Gap Identification & Ideation

P: Plan

5. Focus on the Appropriate Theme
6. Design for legible Circulation
7. Focus on Massing & Volumes
8. Sort out Logical Wet Zoning
9. Design Social Spaces
10. Create Fun Spaces: Café, Break Outs & Recreation Spaces
11. Ensure Support Spaces
12. Design a Variety Of Zones
13. Check on Space Optimisation & Balance Review
14. Ensure a Definitive Colour Scheme
15. Create Multi-Functional Spaces
16. Plan for Future Growth

L: Layer

17. Ensure Security & Safety Compliance
18. Plan for Vibrancy & Buzz
19. Ensure Glocalization thru AV technology
20. Provide for Technology Layering
21. Check Lighting Lux Levels
22. Design for Acoustic Concerns

E: Enable

23. Grow in a Biophilic Approach
24. Manage Sustainability Concerns
25. Ensure Inclusivity in Design
26. Build in Durability & Serviceability
27. Promote Local Art & Artifacts
28. Soften the Workplace Furnishings
29. Plan out Meaningful Signages

X: X Factor: The USP that Sells

Chapter 6

Basic Needs 2: Better Work Space "Process Design"

6.1 Sign Off

6.2 Hand Hold

6.3 Attend Client Concerns

6.4 Persuade & Assure

6.5 Educate the Client

The 10 Points Work space Process Checklist: SHAPE

Management is doing things right; Leadership is doing the RIGHT things!

Peter Drucker

Introduction to Chapter 6:

"To design is much more than simply to assemble, to order, or even to edit: it is to add value and meaning, to illuminate, to simplify, to clarify, to modify, to dignify, to dramatize, to persuade, and perhaps even to amuse. To design is to transform prose into poetry." –Paul Rand

The Last Chapter was all about creating a work space environment that works to create a Positive Work Space Culture & Vibe!

The best of strategies can fail if the right culture is not created; as Peter Drucker has famously said: "Culture eats strategy for breakfast!"

So, getting the Design right is very important.

However, the Design process is Not the END of the process; it's just an Auspicious Start! As we were taught in Architecture School, "There comes a stage when you need to stop Thinking, and start Inking!". The actual Job lies in convincing and materialising a Design into an Actual end product! After all, the proof of the Pudding lies in eating it, not making it!

If the Previous Chapter highlighted the 30 Steps to Design a Great Work Place, this Chapter highlights the 10 Steps or processes to Follow a participative and responsible journey of delivering the same.

Positive Work spaces need to be design with Positive ideation thru a Positive result Oriented process. This section is all about the process an Architect / Interior Designer needs to follow:

6.1 The Sign off

Step 1: Signing Off the Design

A Car is never sold on the basis of a pretty picture or sets of pictures in a brochure; it is sold by showing the real thing: The Car! Work space Design, as all other fields of Creative Design suffers from this issue. Whilst Architectural projects can still rely on hand-made or 3 D printed Models in scale, the fact is that offices are seldom possible to depict thru Physical Models.

Its back then to selling the concept, ideation, design and development thru Plans, sections, elevations and Visualisations. And we expect the Client to be very versatile in understanding what are essentially architects' tools of delivery!

The problems begin, when a design has not been understood and explained properly to a client. The Client relies on his limited exposure to dealing in such projects and only operates on trust and a schematic understanding of things mostly, unless he is a builder or is versatile with the ways of the AEC industry.

Would not life be simpler if designs were not needed to be sold? If Work space architects could do as they wish and everything operated on trust and reputation, as it did in the hey days of Architectural practice?

Unfortunately, as Paul Boag, Leader in user experience Design Thinking, (Boag, 2017) says "Often we win or lose the battle for getting approval before we ever present our work. That is why it is so important to start readying the ground as early as possible".

He further goes on to specify, the four steps:

a. **Define roles up front** (Focus the client on identifying problems that solve the stated demands or problems or fulfil the business goals. And Stress: it is your job to find these solutions.)
b. **Engage and educate often** (Engaging clients in the creation process provides you with an opportunity to educate the stakeholder about your decisions, so that they understand the reasoning behind decisions, and so are more likely they are to approve them.)
c. **Gather your evidence** (Before presenting anything to stakeholders, collect evidence, both qualitative & quantitative, to support your approach. What helps also are stories of earlier user experiences.)
d. **Divide and conquer** (If presenting to many end user stakeholders, it better speaking individually beforehand. That gives a chance to get them onboard informally before the presentation and avoid some of the challenges around group dynamics.)

"How well we communicate is determined not by how well we

say things, but how well we are understood." –Andrew Grove

Recommendations:

I have always followed the few steps below to convince clients and recommend these strongly as well, whilst seeking a sign off:

- Establish your credentials well so they know they are speaking to a person with domain expertise.
- Do the home work of understanding the organisation's corporate journey, so they know you are well informed.
- Keep the presentation crisp and focussed; let them know you have covered all aspects of the brief
- Impress them with the Ideas and Thoughts that cannot be challenged or negated. Justify your design in simple works and logic.
- Focus on the benefits the design will bring to the end users and excite them on the possibilities.
- Assure them that you are a Good Listener; clients hate to be imposed upon. Be Open to critical feedback.
- Do all this humbly, while leaving your ego outside the door; clients get put off by over selling and over display of fame etc.
- Answer their questions, but ask some of yours as well; asking questions reverses the tables and shows you are prepared and involved.

Finally, as Boag rightly says "Success or failure in getting approval for your ideas is about

a lot more than presenting them well. It is about how stakeholders perceive you, what their personal agendas are, the culture of the company and a whole lot besides."

Step 2: Sign offs for Materials & Finishing Sampling

Once a design is signed off, most larger firms invariably feel that the design has been won and relegate the work down the line to the junior designers. This is wrong! Materiality and the sign off of the same is equally important

Materials matter! What gets used and what does not is linked to both "Design Intent" and to "Project Budgets".

Good projects are those that not only get well executed by a good execution team, but those that are well shepherded by the Architect who must ensure the following principles as guidelines to the process:

a. Always identify key aspects of a project leading to Materials that come in the MUST HAVE segment, which you absolutely cannot compromise with. This established the Architects involvement and dominance in the project.
b. Thereafter prioritise the "Should Haves" and the "Could Haves"; Designing is related to Budgeting and is all about prioritisation therein!
c. Adherence to signed off Design Intent is most important: Most Clients rely and trust the shared Animations and renderings; this is where TRUST in Professionals need to

be kept up and samples must adhere to committed look and feel.

d. Adherence to Brand Identity / Corporate Guidelines / Material Play books needs to dovetail into the process; Architects need to set out the parameters of freedom of choice set by these guidelines, instead of assuming limitless freedom and design exuberance!

e. Finally, Materials need to be within Budgets and should not be overtly expensive; neither in currency nor in carbon footprints; it is here that issues of sustainability need to come in; it's better to select Natural materials that are locally sourced instead of flying them in, from around the world.

f. The Pandemic has heightened the seriousness of Good indoor air quality and the criticality of the role mechanical systems play in supporting human health in work spaces. Issues to seek approval also must focus on: MEP systems, MERV filters, UV lighting and the benefits of other healthy building interventions and tools like touchless technology, voice command, anti-microbial surfaces, and smart sensors.

Recommendations:

Few things Architects and Interior designers must remember here:

We are the ONLY Guardians / Custodians of Design! While engineers can run the show, project managers can manage the sites, vendors can submit shop

drawings and detail out intricacies, only an architect can tell and confirm if it all gels well in the end!

This is a Power that needs to be exercised and not abdicated! Architectural experience is needed in Material Selection as much as in other aspects of design and following things are vital to work out for example:

- Does the Material meet the Contextual need of the project and its location?
- What is the manufacturing process of the material and how will it age with time and usage?
- Does any material selected have suitable hardness & durability, under the footfalls anticipated?
- Does a selected material respond well to moisture resistance?
- Are Materials Fire Grade / rated in critical areas?
- Are Tiles too heavy or large to be laid with ordinary cement mix and need chemical adhesives instead?
- Will Partitions be able to carry loads expected off the walls?
- Are Ceilings appropriate to the needs for fire resistance and NRC ratings?
- Are Materials suitable for wet zone or semi-outdoor usage and slip resistant?
- Are wall finishes capable of withstanding boot marks and hand marks?
- Are wall papers vinyl based instead of paper based to withstand temperature changes across seasons?
- Would selected material discolour or fade?
- Are the MEP Planning approaches well-conceived?
- Do they contribute towards a healthier future proof future?

And so much more…

More than anything else, Material Selections can and should be done based on past experiences and precedence.

Step 3: Sign offs for Product Selections:

The Material Selection process is often mixed with the product Selection process, as well. What's the difference, you may ask!? Materials are what you apply on floors, walls, ceiling to put it simply; they are also used in combination to define the Finishes on selected products like furniture, Lounge seating, Lights etc.

Well Material Selections are "Architect Owned and Driven", while Product Selections are "End-User Driven".

Let me explain this:

A Chair may be specified by an architect in terms of style, size, finish, features etc, but it needs to be approved by the end user, as it is he who would sit in it for the rest of the life cycle of the project! The process of selection may be initiated / suggested but cannot (and should not) be enforced beyond a point, wherein ergonomics, lumbar support, material comfort and suitability need participative approval from the client post using for a few days.

Similarly, Work stations, collaborative furniture and other related Products need to be suggested by Architects and approved by the end users / stake holders.

Some aspects of Selection however still remain in the architect's domain for seating of temporary nature such as say Lounge seating, Collaborative furniture, telephone booths, Pods, café seats etc, as these are short duration usage.

But seeking express approval for these is very important and saves a lot of hassles at the end of the day.

Some advice in suitable selection of Chairs and Furniture are as enlisted:

a. Furniture for sitting needs to be chosen based on Ergonomics, features and then looks; often it gets done, in the wrong sequence, leading to problems later on.

b. Furniture for Sitting needs to be flexible, adjustable and supportive of diverse body types; The more possibilities it can cater to adhering to the myriad human forms, that are going to use it, the better.

c. Work station Furniture needs to be chosen on basis of appropriateness to end usage: Does it need to support laptops or desktops or both (along with Monitor arms) decides the depth / width of the work space

d. Work station Furniture also depends on need for access to cabling and connectivity; in an increasing cable free, wi-fi world, this requirement shall reduce; but for present its what decisions are based upon.

e. Work station selection depends upon Flexibility of usage and the need to move it around into various pre-decided configurations, particularly in Training rooms, cafes and other Multi-functional spaces.

f. Lounge Furniture Selection were never made to be comfortable earlier as short usage was encouraged by FM and HR teams; people were wanted back on their assigned desks! All this has changed now in the modern office landscape and comfort and convenience reigns supreme.

g. Connectivity to charging USB points is critical still in new age work lounge furniture and collab points; everything else is related to suitable ergonomics

h. The appropriateness to culture of usage is important to keep in mind; Some cultures do not accept desk-based work stations as easily as partition based, still! Most do not accept work stations and desks without Modesty panels! And few do not accept Lounge seating without back support, as it exposes the back!

Recommendations:

There are certain steps that must be followed for a successful project in the work space domain:

- An early and expedited approval for furniture & other workspace products is important as delivery timelines for unique specs takes longer in a world that manufactures on demand and holds lesser and lesser captive stock.
- Long Lead product Items Include: Chairs, Lounge Furniture, carpets, Lighting and the like that go to make an office
- Establish clarity with the client that while style and functionality would be selected jointly, the look and feel fabrics, finishes, materiality of the products would be in the "Creative Jurisprudence of the Architect"; if not they may please assure that they take the responsibility for the same! (HINT: Nobody argues on issues of Aesthetics with an Architect!)
- It is important to be INVOLVED in this process to establish the INVOLVEMENT in the project and important not to delegate this to other stake holders!

6.2 Handhold (The Client team)

Step 4: Record, Aid & Advise

What has historically been the role of the Architect, must remain to be the Role of the Architect! The Client is the best friend and Elder brother (if you may) for the project realisation and needs to be hand held thru the process of the project.

While this process may have been taken over by project managers, in house Project teams and others, rightfully, as most architects feel it is not their job, my Opinion is that the Architect Must play the Lead rubber stamp role here as well, in the interests of the project!

A Noble profession like Design & Architecture needs to be led at all fronts in order to maintain clarity of thought and leadership thru the project! Too many stake holders and too many ideas often confuse clients and so the Architect has to be the Chief Moderator of his project!

Areas the Architects can Play a Lead role are:

    a. Aiding & Advising on the development of the brief
    b. Aiding & Advising on Either Turnkey Model (Design & Build) or EPC (Engineer, procure & deliver Models)

c. Aiding & Advising on the correct EPC delivery methods: Fixed Lumpsum price, GMP Model, Open Book / cost-reimbursable (also called costs-plus percentage / fixed fee)

d. Aiding and Advising plausible Time Lines for the project given the demands of site, the location, the requirements etc.

e. Aiding and Advising on Prioritisation of Budgets (where to spend and where can cut costs).

f. Aiding & Advising the Right vendors for Multiple items, based on past experiences and deliveries.

g. Aiding & Advising on the best contracting firms for the full part or sub parts of the execution job.

Recommendations:

The Architect Must see himself as the Last man Standing on a ship before it docks (project handover) thru the rough seas and tides and trials and tribunals! He must be the able Captain of the Ship"!

He may not earn or be paid for this, but what he earns in doing so is far more valuable: Moral High Ground and Respect. When this is done, he ensures longevity and connection with the client way beyond one project! In the long run, this pays.

I am a big believer in the King of the Jungle reclaiming his throne in an increasingly VUCA world dominated by everyone now doing "Design and Build" model of work.

Step 5: Update Quality and Progress Reports

The Only person who understands the Vision of the Architect, the realisation of the same and the Detailing is the Architect himself. The Architect needs to be the central Protagonist around him the site revolves. By no means is one referring to a Culture of "Starchitects" as they are infamously called, but there is definitely merit in looking at the Architect as the "Architect Design team".

Lots of time, thoughts and creative energies are invested by teams in coming up with pitches and thereafter finalised schemes and drawings for projects! These are often the results of "nights of work", not just days! Having internalised all that is needed, it is important that a Site is reviewed periodically thru the Architect's eyes / Architect's teams' eyes, ever so often.

The best feedback on progress, quality, clarifications and corrections can originate from an architect's office only! Everybody in the team has a role to play, be it the Creative Design group, the Services Consultants or the Support Acoustic / Lighting Consultant.

Quality and progress need to be Opined by the originators!

Architects Must develop a focus on developing skills of Documentation (and not just drawings) for the purpose of site works evaluations for which they must ensure the following is done:

a. Every site Visit to have an Agenda / Purpose of Visit defined
b. Every Site Visit to be recorded photographically with remarks and sketches for clarifications
c. Every site visit to record key Observations, Decisions & critical comments.
d. Every site visit to document next visit expectations, which form the Agenda for the next visit.

For an architect to do all this, it is important he is paid for project coordination services in addition to Design; often this is neglected, but the best results come on the best sites thru the above simple steps!

Recommendations:

The best way to record Progress and Quality on a site, in the age of amazing hand-held phones and cameras, is to actually walk around site and capture the project thru a Video clip with voice recorded observations that can go back to be formalised into a written documented update.

In the age of Matterport cameras and 3D capturing cameras, it's also good to use these and walk around the site so that the same can be analysed back in the office with the senior members!

Technology has to be an able partner in not just making drawings but in making Site reports as well. Thereafter freeze frames can allow any aspect to be captured and commented upon with ease!

6.3 Attend Client Concerns

Step 6: Manage Change

The Change Management being referred to here is more re the process of managing Change requests from clients / end users, which is the nightmare of most design firms, to be honest. Different firms have different policies on the same with many charging extra hours of work for those changes.

Whatever the case may be, depends on contractual agreements and is not in scope of discussion here; we are here to suggest how to make the process less painful and more productive for everyone!

a. Change requests need to be reasoned as those that are due to non-depiction / explanation by the architect or those that were a change of mind.

b. Once that is clear, clients may be ready to compensate for efforts where change is more of an afterthought, while many may camouflage the same in the first!

c. Change that occurs due to mis-understanding or lack of understanding by the stake holders, may be allowed for; nothing improves relations and trust between an architect and end user than a free and frank appraisal of this "extra work being done at no extra cost!" This prevents any further changes, as clients don't want to feel obliged every time.

d. Any Change, needs to be documented and recorded in a Minutes of Meeting to be shared by the end of the same day. This prevents any further after thoughts or further changes with time!

e. Changes, in orders for Long lead items, may be prevented by seeking signatures on approved samples and holding them in a sample locker.

f. Changes, in requirements, may still come up due to business needs; here the time and cost implications need to be shared up front for the decision to stay or be recused.

g. Changes, in Detailing or site works may be needed from time to time in projects where on-site conditions or expectations may not have been assessed properly; these need to be minimised and handled professionally to get the same end solutions in the best manners possible.

h. Changes, sought at the end of the project, after handover, may be objected to if unacceptable to design architects or accepted if both parties agree to the same. Be true to Yourself and Your Design! The best Doctors are... the best Architects Should!

Recommendations:

In certain parts of the developing world, it is clear that "Client is the King" and so there is abstinence in fighting change, as clients are too powerful! Whilst this is understandable, in some cases, there is need to stand up and exercise the Authority of an Architect as being "First among Equals" in the stakeholders list for a work space design. Few can, few can't.

Step 7: Manage Cost Escalations

Rule No 1: There is No Architect who is perfect and No process that is perfect.

Rule No 2: There is No Client who does not want more and No Architect who does not either, when it comes to a new Work space Design!

RULE 3: Consequently, there is No project that does not have cost Over runs and escalations.

This is Murphy's Law in action: Anything that can go wrong will go wrong!

Often, despite the most conscientious of Cost managers and diligent Project managers who partner architects in projects ranging from a few Million to Multi Million amounts, there are cost over runs and escalations in every project.

Only projects that have built is several layers of buffers, escape this destiny; but that akin to the airlines of the day, that seem to budget in every possible delay in departures and arrivals by adding enough fluff to both ends of the Committed times, creating buffers that are actually misleading in the first place.

Given that there are cost escalations that arise, whether well masked or unmasked, the fact is they need to be dealt with; the best way of which is to do an appraisal mid-way thru the project to ascertain where the project is heading and what can still be done to arrest changes that go beyond the buffers left in "Over heads & Contingencies"! Its like sorting the flight path mid-way thru the flight, rather than leaving it too late to an inevitable delayed arrival!

Recommendations:

Be like a Doctor who informs the consequences of a surgery in full honesty!

Be dead honest with your client; tell him if there are cost escalations and take him into confidence on what are the measures that can help cut back. Concealing or sugar coating erodes the respect and trust of a professional.

Rationalise the Gap Analysis between "estimated and actual costs" logically and apprise where OPEX costs may reduce on account of any CAPEX increases.

Clients are powerful people; they love being explained and assured on ROI's (Returns on Investment).

Whatever the case, keep the Positive Vibe going thru a project!

6.4 Persuade & Assure

Step 8: Involve in Change Management

We spoke of "Managing Change" in its truest sense in Step 6; "Managing the Change" is often called Change management, as well. However, the two are different.

It's quite Simple if you focus on the highlighted Parts:

Managing Change (Step 6) is actually "Change" management and reducing the needs for alterations.

Change Management (here Step 8) is actually Change "Management" wherein you are actually transferring the management from the stake holders to the End users, they represent.

This Step refers to sitting on the same side of the table (for the first time in the project life cycle maybe) as the stakeholders of a new work space project and explaining the changes being planned for the new work space in order to win over the end users.

Change Management, in its true sense, is perhaps the Most Important step that infuses excitement, arouses expectation and Wins over the Positive Mindsets of the potential end users.

While change can be adaptive or transformational, most new work space change management tends to be the latter.

The Harvard Business School outlines (Miller, 2020) Quotes: *"Approximately 50 percent of all organizational change initiatives are unsuccessful, highlighting why knowing how to plan for, coordinate, and carry out change is a valuable skill for managers and business leaders alike."*

It Further elaborates the process of Change Management to have Five Critical Steps:

1. Prepare the Organization for Change

In the preparation phase, the focus is on helping end users recognize and understand the "WHY" for change. They raise awareness of the various challenges or problems facing the organization and generating dissatisfaction with the status quo. Gaining this initial buy-in from employees who will help implement the change can remove friction and resistance later on.

2. Craft a Vision and Plan for Change

Once the organization is ready to embrace change, managers must develop a thorough and realistic plan for bringing it about. The plan should detail:

- Strategic goals: Describing the goals that the change allows achieving.
- Key performance indicators: Defining the units for measuring success.
- Project stakeholders and team: Determining Who will oversee and sign off the changes
- Project scope: defining the steps and actions proposed.

3. Implement the Changes

Post the planning being done, what remains is to ensure the steps outlined, for the change, are followed. Example: changes to the company's structure, strategy, systems, processes, employee behaviours, or other aspects will depend on the specifics of the initiative.

4. Embed Changes Within Company Culture and Practices

Once the change initiative has been completed, the stake holders must prevent a reversion to the prior state or a status quo. This is most important for changes in organisations related to processes, workflows, culture, and strategies. Without "thinking this through" plan, end users may backslide into the "old way" of doing things, particularly during the transitory period.

By embedding changes within the company's culture and practices, it becomes more difficult for backsliding to occur.

5. Review Progress and Analyse Results

Do Note that a change initiative, that is complete may not be one that was successful. Conducting a "project post mortem," can help organisations understand whether a change initiative was a success, failure, or mixed result. It can also offer valuable insights and lessons that can be leveraged in future change efforts.

Recommendations:

The Following Steps can help make the Change Management earlier:

- The end users must be made to see what benefits the change would bring
- The end users must feel empowered, not enslaved with these changes
- The Vision or Dream of what could be as a result of these changes must be amplified
- Potential Roadblocks or stumbling blocks must be anticipated in advance.
- Repeated communication of the organization's vision is critical throughout the implementation process to remind team members why change is being pursued.

Architects MUST be part of this process. A successful onboarding process initiates the employee into the culture and informs them of the alignment with the overall business strategy. This being the key focus of the change management plan, it acts as an effective onboarding document.

6.5 Educate the Client

Step 9: Handle the "Process of Handover"

Handing over requires deft "Handling".

Now here is a perfect analogy everyone will relate to: Think back of the excitement as you are greeted, photographed, and cheered as you take your new car keys from the Sales manager of your favourite car, for which you saved all your money for, for this exact day, of actually driving it out!

Imagine, how it would feel if you arrived to receive your car, the day it was handed over to you, with no one to receive you and nobody to hand hold you thru the last-minute dos and don'ts minutes before you turn on the ignition! It would be a dampener. A Kill Joy.

The Architect needs to turn into the Sales Manager, towards the end of the project and must build a similar sense of achievement and completion, as the analogy!

The Must do Jobs as part of the Handing over process must be:

- A Hand-signed heartfelt note from the architect re-emphasising the Concept of the New Workplace as also thanking all the people who believed in the project and the process!
- A Set of As Built Drawings and Documents Educating the client and the FM teams on all that has gone into the project
- A Documented Listing of all Brands & service providers
- A User's manual with Dos and Don'ts List from all Services Consultants
- A "Lessons Learnt" exercise must be done on handover as well as an audit six months down the line.

Everything else can be handled by more right brained Project managers, whose worthy and handsome contribution in this process is worth applauding and crediting.

Recommendations:

A Handing Over process needs to be similar to letting in your best friend to live in your house while you are away for some time! Alternately, An Architect Must see the Handover process of what was his "erstwhile Child" to the new keepers, in as concerned a manner.

A Good Architect would be proud of this creation and would be ever ready to drop by like an "Indulgent parent" to check on his progeny. Offer this to your client and cement a lifetimes relation!

Step 10: Celebrate Success: "The Joy of Completion"

Whilst this writer subscribes to the theory of evolution and that nothing is ever complete, but is only part of an ongoing process, it's important to celebrate Milestones!

Completing a Project is like reaching a destination; the journey may not be complete, as you embark on the next destination thereafter! But Reaching a Destination is in itself a joy to celebrate and capture.

Most Organisations do not celebrate enough the completion of a project! Architects and Designers must ensure that the "Soul of a Work space" is Celebrated and Elevated with joy and camaraderie.

No matter how much the battles and the bitterness, in some cases, drowning that at the end of the project and letting "bygones be bygones" is appropriate.

There is need for all stake holders to come together and reminisce how the Architect selection was done, how the execution teams were handpicked and how the trials and tribulations of the stake holders were handled.

Reminiscing the key moments of the project journey and the mile stones is a valuable exercise that needs to be done after the project! It's important to discuss the "takeaways and the learnings" of every project, as each project teaches and educates the teacher and the student equally!

Recommendations:

Long lasting relationships and friendships are made on such occasions over an evening, much stronger than the bonds created thru the entire project execution cycle!

The true test of success is when employees express their excitement for their new workplace; Nothing is better music to the ears!

The 10 Step Road map: Work-space Process Checklist: SHAPE

THE SIGN OFF

1. Signing Off The Design
2. Sign Offs for Material & Finishing Sampling
3. Sign offs for Product Selections

HANDHOLD (The CLIENT TEAM)

4. Record, Aid & Advise
5. Update Quality & Progress Reports

ATTEND CLIENT CONCERNS

6. Manage Change
7. Manage Cost Escalations

PERSUADE & Assure

8. Involve in Change Management

EDUCATE THE CLIENT

9. Handle the "Process of Handover"
10. Celebrate Success: "The Joy of Completion"

Chapter 7

Getting IDEOLOGY Right @ Work place

"Companies that invest more in Digital Transformation, actually out-perform their peers over time. These companies are more prepared for disruption, better able to monetize new digital channels, and better able to build a bigger user base. What's more. This phenomenon exists regardless of Industry"

Geoff Cubitt

CEO, Isobar US

Introduction to Chapter 7

The Inverted look at Maslow's Hierarchy of needs has been studied and captured in past chapters, section wise, to an adaptation of modern-day reality at the work place. Post Pandemic, with enough time to ourselves for self-introspection and realisation, our Self-Actualisation / Fulfilment needs are taken care of; Psychological needs are a given; what's left is for the Physiological Environment to be conducive to the New Normal Post the Pandemic! Much has been analysed and much has been recommended.

It has been clearly established that Work place Positivity today is the result of a Positive Work culture & Vibe created in combination of the Right HR & Management Policies together with the Supporting & Conducive Work space Physicality and Materiality!

Cut to 2020-2021:

What are Work space professionals talking about around the world TODAY? What are the new thoughts on what and how the work space needs to be ideated upon from conception to strategy to productivity? How do we get the Ideology Right? This Chapter explores the Most important "SEEDS of THOUGHT" so that "as you sow, so shall you reap!"

The Pandemic and the consequent Work from Anywhere (WFA Culture) has made us sit up and question the new purpose of the office! Whilst all "Pundits of work space" do opine that the Office is not going anywhere, the fact is that new age thoughts and concepts will redefine the way they are ideated. The office will be back, but not in the Pre Covid ways! It will be re-invented and re-purposed into a new reincarnation that will bear little resemblance to how and what we define work spaces as, till now.

This chapter is all about the key concepts that will affect work space ideation of the future!

7.1 The Right Work Space Stake Holders

"No One Can Whistle a Symphony! It takes an Orchestra to Play it"

Halford E Luccock

The First Change is that Successful Work space projects are a Team game! A Team game is different from an Individual sport. All Successful projects are the results of a Joint team Effort by all Stakeholders.

Doing It Right is a team Effort Involving all the Stake Holders: The Architect Team, The Project managers and the Most importantly the Clients. It's a relay Race, where each one needs to run together to make the team win in the end!

Success has many owners, Failure has none! Getting it RIGHT is the Most important aspect for a project as CRE costs are high and moneys invested in New project Fit-outs as well as refurbishments are high. The Stakes are high, deadlines are getting tighter and "Failure is NOT an Option" in today's overtly competitive world!

There is need to understand that all the theories in the world and the best of enumerated practices in SOPS, can go down the drain if they are not followed and not done by the right people! This section is all about getting things right and making sure that "Positive Intent is shown by all Stake Holders to Achieve Positive results"!

There are ways of doing things right and ways of not doing them right! Good projects are the results of Right processes and Approaches. This section is all about that!

The Chapter focuses on the Analogy of an Orchestra and the need to look at the Process of Workplace Design similarly.

A. The Audience (Client)

No orchestra can perform without an Audience; it can practice, but it needs an Audience to perform for and perform to! To seek appreciation and to seek applause is what an artist lives for! So does a Work Space designer, with the right attitude: he loves for the appreciation of the end user group!

The Audience / The End User are similar beings: they trust you and provide you their time and their attention to your creativity. They

need to be thanked as well and their contribution needs to be appreciated as well. The Bigger the Audience, the Bigger the stage, the bigger the performance!

Good work space design is similar; it starts and ends with the Client! The Right kind of client is what every architect dreams for! After all, not every type of audience likes every type of music! So, what defines the right kind of audience for a work space Design or any creative work?

Indeed, there was a time when the reverse would happen; where the Client used to check out and examine the credentials of the architect much before considering, which led to the elaborate process of PQ (Pre-Qualification) for Architects and others in the AEC segment. Today, it's a two-way street; the Clients also need to be Pre-Qualified & carefully Selected!

Let's analyse what one looks for in a Client? Forbes Agency Council (Council, 2017) is an invitation-only community for executives in successful public relations, media strategy, creative and advertising agencies. It may not be Architectural Design, but it's still relevant! It has published 10 very interesting Attributes list from 10 people on the Forbes Council, that are selectively borrowed from:

1. Cooperation

"Easy is overrated; the only difficult client is a client who thinks we can make them successful, without their help. But we can't work in a vacuum. So sometimes, finding balance and flow, with a client, can take a while because everyone has a different way of working. The ideal client has clear goals and a picture of how

to get there. And he / she trusts us to deliver our part of the journey." - Jean-Luc Vanhulst, Write2market, Inc.

2. Fairness

"If clients embrace the characteristic of fairness, agency life is much easier. It's quite simple. For example, it's fair to ask for a change order when the scope of work has increased significantly due to client needs. If a client embraces a fair mindset, they will be reasonable and understanding in why they should authorize the change order." - Craig Cooke, Rhythm

3. Passion

"Aside from the ability to keep clear lines of communication open, the thing that makes for an enjoyable experience is working with a business owner who is genuinely passionate about their business. These business owners know their customers, they know their products or services inside and out, and they just enjoy what they do. Marketing campaigns are always fun with these types of customers." - Vinny La Barbera, im FORZA

4. Honesty

"Whether it's bad news or good news, I want to hear it from my clients. Budget cuts, focus changes, new hires, missed deadlines – whatever it is, it must be communicated. I know too many great agencies that lose a customer simply because the communication halted. Great agencies will overcome any change, given the opportunity to serve their client." - Douglas Karr, DK New Media

5. Comfort With The Uncomfortable

"The idea of change or innovation in the abstract always sounds like a good idea, but when it comes time to execute, clients often panic. Sure, it's challenging to pivot your way of thinking or

experiment in the unknown, but without doing so, you can never truly innovate." - Dan La Civita, Firstborn

6. A Sense Of Humor

"Can you joke with them? Give them a hard time? Tease them? Have a good laugh together? Let your guard down? Relax? Be yourself? All these things build trust and a relationship built on honesty. Humour cuts to the chase. If you can laugh at the same things, you have common ground to build on." - Randy Hughes, Carmichael Lynch

7. A Teamwork Mentality

"Too often we see potential clients with an "us" versus "them" mentality; this never works. Unless we all realize and appreciate that we are in this and need to work together for maximum success, it usually won't work. Having a true teamwork mentality makes clients' success that much greater. We seek out these types of clients and they are truly enjoyable to work with." - Duree Ross, Durée & Company

8. Trust

"The best relationship a client and a firm can have is a trusting relationship. The client needs to take on a firm that he has received good references for and has good chemistry with. Once that firm has been hired, give them your trust. Don't doubt them. Enable them to do their job in the best way possible and they will. That's what you hired them for." - Ayelet Noff, Blonde 2.0

While this may be generic, there is need to define the perfect client! Years of Working in this domain have taught me the key attributes of a GOOD CLIENT to be as under:

1. One Who Trusts you!
2. One who you can trust!

3. Ones who have realistic Expectations (Time & Budgets)
4. Ones who also listen and ready to take advise.
5. Ones who are involved and are a SPOC
6. Ones who participate, but do not Over dominate
7. Ones who pay on Time!

These are the compelling truths for the Industry & while anyone may work with anyone, there is all sorts of music as well... But not all music is appreciated and makes it to the charts!

B. The Conductor (Architect)

A Good Orchestra is orchestrated by the Conductor; the leader of the Pack is the Architect. Finding the right architect is the Most essential aspect for a Good Work space design, is a no brainer. Yet, in an increasing VUCA world, with more choice and more availability of professional architects, Turnkey Contractors, Aggregators and all, the choice is not often so simple.

Selection procedures normally vary across different sectors: Public, Private and Individual segments. However, if there would be an ideal SOP, this could be it:

Step 1. Establish Pre-Qualification / Evaluation Criteria

- These criteria are to evaluate the general information for the architect's background and experience, as well as the specific proposal developed for your project.
- The Prospective architects must be Experienced and conversant with the project Typology and should meet pre-qualification requirements.

This does not mean that young architects be side lined; there is great talent that needs to be given opportunity to record their first!

Step 2. Invite Short-listed Architects

- Invite proposals from the firms to understand their past work and their vision for the Work spaces.
- Review the evaluation criteria received from the short-listed architects.

Step 3. Short-list Architects based on Proof Of Concept Submissions / Part Design

- Set Up Criteria for evaluation of key Concepts / ideation where applicable: Both Commercial & technical.
- Review the same, with due weightage to both commercial and technical inputs; also review past credentials and Jobs done, keeping an eye open for new talent as well.

Step 4. Conduct Interviews

- Use evaluation criteria to guide process and develop preliminary ratings; seek interviews with principals to understand and connect with the vision of your prospective architect.
- Also, ensure interviews with the assigned teams from the firms, that you will actually be working with.

Step 5. Consider a Mentor Architect to Guide

- Often the choice of the most appropriate architect may need to be guided by a qualified mentor / Past Architect who can help identify the one most suited.
- Architects Must be conversant with the scale and complexities of the job, having done a few similar projects; There may be young architects with the right intent and skills, but lacking the experience; so, the decision needs to be guided by a mentor.

- There could also be a case for concept design being done by an experienced firm that is not local, with a local firm doing the design coordination and contract administration.

Step 6. Negotiate Contract

- Begin negotiations with the highest ranked firm based on qualifications. If negotiations fail, go on to the next highest ranked firm. Do not make decisions ONLY on the basis of Least Fee quoted! There are umpteen examples of increased costs thereafter towards corrections, after selecting a wrong architect!
- Make the decision within the time frame and make public the award of the same to avoid complexities that arise due to word of mouth.
- Send polite regret notes that thank and acknowledge the efforts of the other competing firms; this process is normally forgotten in the present day fast paced world and is an absolute must.

It is recommended to look for an architect principal, who is fired up for your project and has the absolute hunger and desire to perform, lead & guide his team "personally" on the project. Too often, works are awarded to principals, who then vanish

from the scene to only handover the projects to lesser competent persons in the team.

Getting the right Team of Architects for a project should be the most important FIRST STEP towards achieving a work space design that works for the organisation. Selection of the right architect is as important as choosing the right direction towards a destination!

"A **doctor can bury his mistakes**, but an architect **can** only advise **his** client **to** plant vines." — Frank Lloyd Wright

C. The Orchestra (The Build Team)

An Architect can only make wonderful plans, coordinate the works and make pretty pictures; but all this can go down the drain if the selection of the Build Partner is wrong! The Right Build Partner can make or break a project! It is important that the process, of selecting a contractor, is also referred to the Architect and Appointed project managers.

A Great evaluation technique for contractors (apart from their meeting the established PQ Criteria, mentioned earlier for architects as well) is the method consisting of 5 P's: **People, Process, Portfolio, Price** and **Past Clients**.

Based on a Post (unknown, HOW TO SYSTEMATICALLY CHOOSE THE RIGHT CONTRACTOR, Unknown) these, you can create a 0–50 ranking system that drastically reduces the risk of ending up with the wrong contractor and throwing your money down the drain. The first step is to narrow down your choices of contractors to a manageable number. Here, 3-5 is ideal. These final contenders can be found by asking friends and family for referrals and selecting those in your local area.

PEOPLE: People with the Right Attitude, Skills and Knowledge are the key here; does your first meeting impress you? Do you instinctively feel the right or wrong noises? A lot depends on this. A Project is alike a marriage and needs to have the right suitors for the period.

PROCESS: Understanding the "HOW" is the most important aspect of the interactions. How will the contractors execute the job withing the given time period and budgets? How will he manage it? How will he be personally involved? How will the project reporting be done? How will he deal with emergencies? How will he deal with project over runs on committed items of work? How will he take up aspects of the job that are challenging? How will he best understand the design intents as specified by the architects? Often, these may sound basic questions, but often they do not get asked...with tragic results later.

PORTFOLIO: Most Contractors may commit the moon when taking on a project but will need to be asked to share past works done of similar nature to best call their bluff (if any). The fact remains that vast sums of money are committed in projects and so the system of selection of the appropriate contractor must hinge on their past work and the quality of the same. Contractors are mostly evaluated on the basis of their familiarity with the type of work done and their quality of works delivered.

PAST CLIENTS: Despite all of the above, past referrals are most important to evaluate the past performance and delivery of the contractors are very much needed to be evaluated. Good referrals provide an assurance and tantamount to a certificate of ability, that cannot be ignored.

PRICE: And Finally, it all boils down to PRICE! The best contractor may still need to quote reasonably to win a project; a quote is often seen as an expression of interest! A Good Competitive quote indicates a high desire to work, while a high price is often a signal of disinterest.

Contractors MUST NOT, however, be selected solely on price. The Lowest quote is often a temptation, but it is also laced with the danger of unimaginable extras and unforeseen items that may come up. Contractors with good scores in all the other "P's" will not be cheap; so, awarding to the cheapest is often at the peril of all other criteria mentioned.

The best of architects cannot extract work out of run of the mill contractors who quote low to win the job! This is where the client has to be discerning!

A Good orchestra needs to have the best team of players who work in tandem and in rhythm to each other, following the baton of the conductor to please the audience!

7.2 The Right Work Culture

Positive Work Places are all about the need to create a "Vibe and an Ambience of a Certain Type" that defines the heart and Soul of a Work Place! It's the intangible feel of a place that greets you from the point of entry and escorts you in through all the spaces and expresses itself to varying degrees!

Culture is Everything! As Dr Peter Drucker says "Culture Eats Strategy for Breakfast!"

Workplace culture is the environment that you create for your employees. It is the mix of your organisation's leadership, values, traditions, beliefs, interactions, behaviours and attitudes that contribute to the emotional and relational environment of your workplace.

Rosie Ward (Co- Author of HOW to Build a Thriving Culture at Work) explains the connection of Culture and Wellbeing and the importance for leadership to bridge the two. "It's all about Leaders having a Mindset of valuing employees, really understanding the importance of Organisation Culture and recognizing that Wellbeing is a piece of the total employee experience". (Putnam, 2015)

Positive Actions and Positive Attitudes make for a Positive Work Culture; Often thru Collaboration and Communication it is possible to create this vibe. This needs to percolate thru and thru a work space; it's not possible to have this only on certain floors or certain departments. Work Culture is a Vulture that cannot be chained to any one part! Its either there throughout or not there at all.

Why do some places have this Positive Work Culture that is most recognisable and many do not!?

As per a Forbes paper by Dr Pragya Aggarwal (*Inclusivity Consultant, Behavioural Scientist, TEDx Speaker, Author of SWAY: Unravelling Unconscious Bias*) "key research by Deloitte has shown that 94% of executives and 88% of employees believe a distinct corporate culture is important to a business' success. Deloitte's survey also found that 76% of these employees believed that a "clearly defined business strategy" helped create a positive culture." (Aggarwal, 2018)

There are several ways a Positive Work Culture can be achieved:

It starts with the "**Mission and Vision statement**" of an Organisation; the values it creates that need to be followed at a work place. This is what was referred to as the very "Ikigai or Purpose" at the organisation level that needs to be communicated down to the employees.

Positive Work Culture also seems to have its roots from the "**Leadership & Management style**" adopted in the office. The more carefree and relaxed the Leadership and Management style, the more dynamic and vibrant is the work culture. The much-understated phrase "Lead by Example" is a clear way to instil this sense of Positivity in a work place! It's a Top Down Process that must permeate down to all the echelons of the organisation.

The "**Open and Honest Communication Style**" is most vital to the creation of a Positive Feeling in the workplace; it promotes a sense of freedom and upliftment that very little else does!

An "**Inclusive Work Environment**" where freedom for all types of gender, economic strata, orientation and colour is part of the work place ethic, contributes massively to a sense of Positivity in the work space environment.

Finally, The Work culture of a space can be enhanced by creating "**Defined Goals and Rewards**" for employees that allow for greater initiative, commitment and "Do or Die" spirit.

It is an amazing and eye-opening fact that the changes in management and direction, that are common to all the points above, can make for a Positive work place! It's often linked to the personality, educational back ground and exposure of the leader of a single owner driven office! New Age Start-ups mostly imbibe these values more out of need to attract and retain employees than anything else.

The benefits of adopting these approaches are: Greater sense of pride, attachment and commitment to an organisation! This leads to a greater motivated and engaged workforce that leads to a greater productivity and growth of the organisation! Anything that benefits the growth and sustainability of a workplace is gold dust! This is where HR and Management is increasingly becoming most important in shaping new age work forces!

In that sense a Positive work place culture is an important recruitment advertisement for most organisations that embrace this change in ethos as a fundamental way of making a for a different work place that attracts and retains!

> **While we often say we are creatures of habit, we are really creatures of culture!" as per Laura Putnam, Author of Workplace Wellness that works. At the heart of a Great Culture is a Highly engaged Employee. (Putnam, 2015)**

Culture shapes the Destiny of a Work place and is the Number one Point to ideate upon!

7.3 The Right Identity V/s Aspirations Debate

There are Three Types of Companies in my observation: The Multi-generational established companies, the First generational growing Companies and the newly spouted Start-Ups.

Most Companies, more so the established ones, have a distinct sense of Corporate identity enshrined in brand manuals and corporate identity documents from the beginning. This is particularly relevant in companies that have progressed from one generation to another and have been able to review their Vision statement (V), Mission statement (M) and Goals (G) objectively over time! The Corporate identity" or "Branding" simply evolves from the V, M & G statements!

Other first generational companies are always in a state of growth and are wanting to embrace better ways of functioning and branding, so as to be able to create better retention and lower attrition. These companies and organisations are always ready to challenge pre-set notions and discard them for something better that meets their current aspirations and purposes!

The Start-ups are the ones that are MOST Fluid in their corporate identity and often suggest that they are a "Work In progress"! Being the most Open and most receptive, they allow for a freer and more open dialogue in establishing what works and what does not for them!

The Work place Design is mostly defined by understanding how much a company wants to bend the rules and operate within the grey areas of a defined Corporate identity!

There have been instances of rigid abiding by Corporate Guidelines that tend to yield a standard result in the workplace design, where in context, location and people are less important than the enshrined Brand identity. Instances of such rigidity are only reducing in present times, with people valuing the need for a "Contextual Approach" and "Adaptive Tinkering" within the confines of set parameters.

And then there have been the odd instances where an entire new office designed by us for an Indian origin MNC has gone and changed its very logo and corporate identity based on the new office interiors created!

There have been cases where a design for a reception table has become so iconic that it has gone into the brand manual internationally! While such cases may be few and far between, they do indicate a growing receptiveness to change and newer ideas! This should encourage designers to question and constantly tweak beyond what they are handed down!

There have also been instances where having adhered to strict guidelines of corporate identity, the offices have relaxed the norms in subsequent additions and expansions, keeping in mind feedbacks from the user work force. Yes, democracy at work place exists and more and more managements are forced to listen to their most valuable assets: their work forces, about "what should be and what shouldn't be" in their work places!

It is this sort of dialogue and debate between inherited Corporate identity and user aspirations that is a sign of how "ALIVE" the organisation really is! Organisations that allow for this freedom of expression embracing local culture, values and end user peoples' tastes, knowingly or unknowingly, create a greater sense of attachment to the new work spaces!

7.4 The Right Future Proof Way of Working: Agility & ABW

Let's Understand these Two concepts that often are wrongly synonymous for many!

Agile workplaces (or Smart Working) are spaces that are designed for maximum flexibility. They empower employees to work however, whenever and wherever, they choose to and from! Whether in office or Out of Office, Agility embraces Choice and flexibility!

An agile work culture focuses more on finding the best way to solve a problem rather than applying the same procedural approach to every situation. This flexibility applies, not just to how work is done, but also to the work environment is itself! Work can now be done from a high counter, a booth, a café seat, a meeting room, focus room, pod or even from the desk....rather than ONLY from the erstwhile desk!

The Very CHOICE and FLEXIBILITY in how we choose to work and when we choose to work and where we choose to work is a Game Changer! It is empowering, fulfilling, engaging and productive both at the Individual as well as at the Organisational level. This Autonomy is liberating and maximises the work potential, especially, for the Millennial.

The advantages of Agility:

- Greater sense of autonomy and freedom for employees
- Job satisfaction, leading to better engagement and talent retention
- Overall reduction in operating costs

The challenges for Agility:

- Calls for a major culture shift for both, employees and management
- Can't be applied selectively; the entire business needs to buy into the concept
- Requires smart technology and supporting IT infrastructure

Activity Based Work, on the other hand, allows for a range of activities, from individual focus work to ideation (independently or in teams), collaboration on content or knowledge sharing; thereby giving each person the freedom of choice to decide how they work to achieve the best versions of their outputs!

Like Agile Working, Activity Based Working also allows employees the freedom to choose how they wish to work. However, that's where the similarity ends.

Whereas, Agile Working is all about the individual employee, the fact is that Activity Based Working is more about teamwork and group culture. Here a lot of importance is given to changing workplace culture and design to suit team connections and to foster collaboration.

The advantages for ABW:

- This offers employees a choice of different workspaces

- There is greater autonomy for employees which gives them a chance to perform at their best
- Employees are more engaged and there is definite improvement in productivity

The challenges for ABW:

- Does not work with every type of industry or job role
- Requires a major shift in office work culture and management techniques
- Could entail physical re-structuring of workspaces

The fact remains that the Pandemic has forced on us an adoption of an Agile "SOLO" work experience that makes for working from wherever, whenever and however, so long as the Job gets done! Offices have, unwantedly, been forced to accept the reality that life (read work) can go on this way, without major drops in performance or efficiency, as feared before.

However, Activity based Work is the future for most organisations that entail working together in closer physical collaboration! So, when offices would re interpret their ideologies and ikigai, they will consider offices to be more Activity / team based, as Agile / Solo working can be done from anywhere!

The Future beckons to a more inclusive way of working! Agile work would need to be accepted as the "new normal" with Offices being designed for more Activity based work approaches!

As a result, offices may become smaller and accommodate for the probabilities of a Roster based work approach that will enable a 50-60% holding capacity at any time! Offices may also become more neighbourhood based to reduce commutes and travel times to distant central locations!

Office space optimization software is also called room and resource management software. This is what allows organizations to both optimize their spaces and provide employees with a productive, collaborative experience.

These enable employees to:

- Book workspaces or schedule instantly or in advance thru web, mobile, calendar and on-the-spot access points.
- Find spaces by capacity, in-room technology (e.g., video conferencing) and geographic location.
- Select favourite spaces for quicker reservations.
- Avoid room and resource conflicts that throttle productivity and create friction.

Optimizing office space, through flexible floor plans and scheduling technology, not only gives employees greater satisfaction and the ability to work the way they prefer, but also helps companies increase their employee-to-desk ratio, ultimately reducing their CRE costs, operational costs and increasing the return on facilities investments.(Carter, 2020)

The future beckons to being alive to these new age concepts of the past decade that are now seemingly more relevant in a Post pandemic world!

7.5 The Right Numbers Game

How often have we heard somebody smart say " It's all in the numbers!"? And, while this may be a common comment in a CA office, it has great bearing on how work spaces are designed as well! The numbers refer to the head count and to the densities achieved on the floor plates, and the ratios therein, that allow for optimal functioning for each domain or department type.

How come some offices look dull and desolate? Other seem to be brimming with activity and engagement? How come some work spaces have a buzz around them that is infectious and contagious to the spirit! There is either a positive buzz or a negative vibe to a work place that has to do with the numbers on the floor!

The truth: what makes a world of difference in Office Design is getting the right mix ratio or the right density that meets different requirements. It is here that certain key criteria need to be analysed:

A. The Business case: there is a certain minimum threshold needed to do an activity or do run a business! It may be 10 employees for a small organisation and maybe 100 in a larger office area. In any case, as per Gallup's State of the American Work place "only 30% employees are actively committed to doing a good job in any office" and can this be considered the core! Whatever the number, the business case will decide what is needed on minimum.

B. The Target Output: the size of an office also depends on the workforce needed to complete a task and ensure that all aspects of a business are covered thru the teams, performing or non performing!

C. The work environment: to few companies, the numbers also depend on the intangible feel of how bustling and energetic the work place must be! This is mostly the only foothold a designer or architect has to interpret and advise a client. The other two are not in his hand.

The magic of a work space that is "happening" depends on this mix ratio or density! There is a fine line between optimum and over packed densities. Most wars between designers and FM / HR teams from the client-side are on these numbers! CRE is expensive and the natural inclination is to pack up spaces till the rafters. This is where an architect needs to use his skills and expertise to ensure that it's not over packed or over dense.

Most bustling, Asian metropolitan cities have the need for higher densities, akin to the streets, the offices are located off! It's funny, the denser the surroundings, the denser the interior spaces are planned. Space index seems to be tighter in cities like Mumbai and Kolkotta, than say Delhi or Bangalore!

While we subconsciously fight with the crowds inside the office in many cases, in others, where the densities are lesser, we are trying to bring in the bustle and buzz of the streets, into the offices, thru various ways!

There is a crazy relationship between age group of end users and densities! Lower the user age group, more are the densities, as

seen in call centres and online tech offices. Higher the age group of end users, lower is the density on the work floor, as seen in consulting or legal firms.

Densities of offices are mostly 1 person per 100 sft (pre-pandemic) to 1 in 150 sft (post pandemic) in mature offices with mature age groups. And on the other end of the spectrum, densities can also be 1 in 50 (pre and post pandemic!) for offices with younger age groups and worker profiles.

The ideal target is around 75 to 80 sft to a person! This achieves a balance of good space utilisation and getting the right buzz! Caution: This may vary from geographies & contexts.

The ideal meeting seat per headcount in office is 1 meeting seat per 10 user seats in more collaborative offices to 1:20 in others.

The ideal cafe sizing for offices is 1 cafe seat for every three to maximum 4 people, enabling lunch in 3 to 4 shifts respectively.

The ideal collaboration seat per headcount is 1:10 to 1:20, depending upon how much collaboration is needed in the nature of work the office does!

All these numbers change when newer age concepts of Agile or Activity based work come into play! Then, it's more the feel and the vibe of a place that's best decided by an architect, based on context, demographics, location of CRE and other factors! It's best to leave certain grey areas so that workspace architects can interpret freely! After all, designing work places that work is part art as well as part engineering.

An Interesting study (Wernick & Morris, 2020) also talks about companies having three types of employees: Anchors, Connectors and Navigators.

'Anchors': The Resident Office Workers

Anchors spend much of their time in-office. They are very autonomous and rarely leave their personal work settings or immediate surroundings. Anchors may be fixed to a certain location and may require access to in-office resources like paper files.

'Connectors': The Hybrid Workers

Connectors have a hybrid work schedule, spending part of their time remote and part in-office. Many employees have proven they can be productive remotely, and we believe that the hybrid work model will become more commonplace than ever before. Connectors come into the office regularly for specific tasks that can't be done (or can't be done as well) remotely. They are mobile while in the office, moving around to different spaces based on the task at hand.

'Navigators': The Remote Workers

Navigators are highly mobile, and their work can be done anywhere. Navigators rarely use the office, accessing it to exchange information and attend meetings. They come to the workplace as needed, which could be a few days per month for a strategic brainstorming session or an all-hands event. Since these worker types interact with the office in different ways, there are distinct combinations of the New Workplace Kit of Parts that support them best.

What a wonderful new office landscape are we all going to enter into in the Post Pandemic !

7.6 Doing It Right: The Digital Workplace

> **"After a year of research, surveys, interviews and analysis, we can state with confidence, that we will never return to what most people considered 'normal' at the beginning of 2020," said JLL Senior Director of Research Christian Beaudoin. "The world has evolved and accelerated in ways that will alter our future and there is no going back."**

So says a report from JLL (release, 2021)

The Digital Work Place is the new Normal, that was reinforced by the Lock downs and made to be the way of the future, irrevocably.

Unlike the "Traditional Workplace" that was a physical environment, the digital work place is Virtual. It is "Online", not "Offline", as most businesses were in the past, pre covid. It is "Cloud based" and Not "server based". It is "anywhere", not anywhere.

The best lines by a recent posting in WORK DESIGN Magazine (Miscowich & Puybaraud, 2021) say it all: **In a post-pandemic world, work is no longer somewhere you go, but something you do.**

Infact, the Pandemic has accelerated workplace trends that were already underway, from digitally transformative business models to prioritizing employee health, wellness and experience anywhere, where work happens. But, even more profoundly, the disruptions of the past year have irrevocably changed perceptions of work itself, for companies as well as its employees.

"What is Work" and "Why is the Work Place Relevant today" are questions that come up in Most webinars and discussions to date!

What has happened is that the "future of work" has arrived far earlier than anyone even expected. Trends that were anticipated to take years to materialize have already reached mass adoption and there is no going back. The myth, that "work-from-home" models cannot work, has been shattered and "work from anywhere" is now the new normal.

Where you are working from is no more relevant! "Are you working & meeting your targets" is far more important. Work is now Target based and not supervised or monitored. People can now be anywhere in the city or the country (or the world) and can still be connected virtually and not feel hampered from being away from their physical work place destinations of the recent past!

The changing notion of work is changing concepts and strategies for CRE (Corporate Real Estate) and is already leading to newer priorities and opportunities for workplace leaderships to redefine the work, the workforce, and the definition of workplace success. Lots of new Questions!

The Questions are: do we go back to the past or do we embrace the new normal? Disruption has been the key word! When do we get back to "normal" has been the typical Question! "The New Normal" has become the new Phrase for everyday life. The mask has replaced the new handkerchief, as you leave home for anywhere.

To achieve the best of a "work-from-anywhere approach" & maximising human experience, while optimizing real estate and technology investment—organizations must rethink some foundational questions, including:

- How is work performed, and where and when does it happen?
- What are employee preferences, and how are people performing?
- What should be the size and location of the future workplace, one that enables a workforce to adopt emerging "hybrid" work-from-anywhere workplace behaviours?
- How can we provide authentic and deep human connections, enhanced collaboration and improved cognitive performance with individual places to concentrate?

But, it's been widely acclaimed to have also been a "Good Virus" that questioned of our wasteful ways of burning energy and money to commute long distances to work, pollute cities in doing so and repeat while coming home. Besides the wastage of time, the waste of physical and emotional energy is also not to be forgotten.

The new Digital transformation allows to pick and choose, where to work, from, a much larger canvas, than ever before. If you are under the weather, no problem, you could work from home, at your own times and your own pace. No absenteeism anymore; only work targets with greater flexibility and responsibility!

The roadmap to a new and better normal, is not simple. Workplace leadership would need to embrace bold, new ways that would allow for meaningful new employee preferences. That begins with exploring how your organization relates to key new themes in the world of work, including the ones at play now, and what to anticipate in the years ahead.

Digital transformation and sustainable strategy go hand in hand. As per the research paper (Miscowich & Puybaraud, 2021) "Advancing connective technology has proven urgently essential in keeping projects moving during COVID-19, but the benefits of these and other digital investments will outlive the pandemic. Leaders who bring employees into a digital-first world, while keeping human experience front and center, can capitalize on these advances, to inspire and engage their workforce and thrive in the new future of work. Today, that means immersive digital collaboration, virtual office experiences and more, and may soon include augmented, mixed, extended and virtual reality along with advanced telepresence technologies."

It's been predicted by the Pundits: "2025 and Beyond will Embrace a "Work-from-Anywhere" Culture as the high-performance path forward"!

The opportunity to shape the future of work has never been more real. Workplace leaders who explore innovative ways of working to deliver high-quality memorable moments for people—wherever they may be working—can help shape a more responsible and resilient world of work leading up to 2025, and beyond.

7.7 The Notion of "The Work Club"

Make no mistake about it! The Work space will remain but will reincarnate into a new being!

The fact is the pandemic has entailed a new possibility of WFH, but people do not want to work from home, for many reasons and actually, prefer coming back to their offices. In fact, WFH is giving way to WFA (Work from Anywhere) which could also mean a satellite office or a coffee shop; but people need people and want to get out of the confines of WFH.

According to recent research (Miscowich & Puybaraud, 2021), "66 percent of employees are expecting to be able to work from different locations post-crisis, yet 74 percent of employees still want the ability to come into an office. Their reasoning varies, but 70 percent find that the office environment is more conducive to team building and management support, while 49 percent are expecting socialization spaces to boost their experience in the office."

The Work-space needs to re-engineer itself as a "melting pot" or "meeting point". We are now beginning to hear different names to it, from different corners of the Post Pandemic World:

- The Work-space as a "**Collab Hub**": where socialising spaces are primary and everything else is supporting cast!
- The Work-space as a "**Social Café**": One where you go for good coffee and some work!
- The Work Place as "**The Market Place**": where one meets to transact, buy and exchange ideas and concepts!
- The Work-space as a "**Work Club**": one you go to three days a week!
- The Work-space as a "**Work Hotel**": where you check in for the day and check out when your tasks are complete!
- The Work-space as an "**Innovator's Guild**" looks at the work space as a place people go at their leisure to innovate and exchange!

A Wonderful report entitled "Working Better Than Normal; Vision 2021" by JLL (Ryan, 2021) describes how people would like to see the future work place! Would you not call this a CLUB?

An exciting post written recently best describes the new turn-around (Zak, 2021):

"The Innovator's Guild resembles social clubs of the past – inspiring and stimulating environments where members pay to have access to the space itself and the other members in the group. Eliminating the elitism associated with social clubs, our depiction is an environment that is exclusive rather than exclusionary. Rather than the silly concept of charging employees to use the office space, the Innovator's Guild is part of the employment package. It is a place the employee always has access to, more like a work perk. So how does this rebranded office look?"

Nicole Zak (Zak, 2021) best describes the five "MUST HAVE'S" that make up the Innovator's Guild:

1. **A Hospitable Co Working Space:** *"...where there is a dedicated concierge for occupants offering coffee, dry cleaning, food delivery, and mailing and shipping services. It's a place where employees can go to receive modern-day "white glove" service they aren't getting from home, drawing them back into the office more often."*

2. **A High Tech Production Suite:** *"...where it's like a one-stop shop for printing, copying, designing, and producing. There are high-tech, easy-to-use Zoom suites where employees can go for uninterrupted, seamless virtual meetings."*

3. **An Amenity Driven Retreat:** *"... with unlimited access to fitness and wellness amenities, including an app-based fitness center equipped with the newest smart home gym equipment that people don't have room for in their homes. Other wellness features include modern salt rooms, meditation rooms, spas, biophilic design elements, and sensory rooms, going beyond just physical health by making mental health a priority.*

4. **A Connection Alcove:** *"...It is a place for connection, engagement, and innovation. Multi-purpose rooms and social spaces will take on a new role as event spaces for employees and the community. These areas will also be*

more accessible than ever before, inviting employees and their friends and families to enjoy the office's perks after hours and on the weekends."

5. **A Welcoming Union:** *"...where everyone feels at home and has the freedom to decide their work style. A place where all voices are heard, and both choice and trust are placed on a pedestal. It's a place where nine-to-five visibility no longer equals productivity. Instead, workers can take advantage of what the office offers and how it helps them accomplish their tasks."*

What emerges in all this, is the advent of a Hospitality Angle to the work space: The new work place needs to be more "privileged" by being: more inviting, more hospitable, more engaging and more enabling than ever before. Work can happen, but it's more about Physical interaction, engagement and collaboration!

Its also about conveniences:

With the New "work place" being redefined as the new "meeting place" or "Club" for like-minded people who happen to work in the same organisation and need to interact, there is need for re calibration.

Previously one used to "Work from HOME", but now the concept emerges to "Home from WORK"! How can the new Work place be more home like? How can it be more Resimercial (Part Residential & Part Commercial)? How can we be made to "Feel at Home" in the return to offices, is one of the most consuming questions for most organisations.

Indeed, this trend, toward a home-like workplace, comes from the increasing desire of people to work remotely from home. However, working remotely from home, is generally at odds with upper management, still and in emerging economies in particular. Therefore, many managers and executives are now choosing to design their workplaces to be so comfortable and home-like, that employees would want to stay in the office for as long as possible.

That's where the Physical space settings and the space attributes need to be re questioned and re-purposed. It's also important for the work space to provide amenities that are convenient for the end user

- High back lounge chairs, sofas with rugs, lamps and accessories that resemble home are the new normal.
- Greenery, Pots and plants add a homely feel.
- Art works and eclectic touches of art pieces in work spaces are the new way ahead!
- Cafes and Break out areas with Premium Coffee, Packed food and fruits
- Outdoor terraces and balconies
- Exercise Gyms & Showers
- Meditation spaces & Quiet Rooms
- Mothers' rooms and Creches

It's a worker-centric world, after all. To ignite performance, many businesses are reinventing their practices around productivity, flexible working, recruitment, and becoming closer aligned with the workforce. At the same time, positive employee experiences have become critical to business performance.

Many thoughtful workplace leaders are now deepening their resolve to champion human experience programming through health and well-being amenities, inclusion and diversity initiatives, and experiential workplace features.

The speed of the trend toward hybrid work is likely to increase, with a repurposed workplace at its core.

Home like work spaces are definitely more productive as they are more engaging. They stimulate a sense of being carefree and casual, instead of the formal offices of the past! The Offices are less intimidating, less perfect and less formal. In such relaxed settings, there is greater expression of thoughts, innovations and ideation!

"In a hybrid workforce world, it's not only about the plexiglass. It's about the person." Says Laura Vierling (Vierling, 2021)

Increasingly Much is being said and talked about the new landscape and the emergence of this New Work place that is actually seen to be a saviour or a vaccine to the way we were working before the virus struck, ironically.

This new work place, best described by a Post (Insights, 2021) titled "The Future Workplace: Top 10 predictions" alludes to a world that will be different:

1. ***Remote work is here to stay.***
   Remote work desires are (and have been) growing. Organizations are preparing to meet this demand, and future competition for talent will take place over the battlegrounds of not just flexible work policies, but also flexible work support such as stipends, home office equipment, and technologies. Organizations will also need to focus on maintaining and strengthening their culture for remote employees.

2. ***The office is here to stay, too.***
   The physical office still has a role to play even in a more mobile future, but it will be designed to support flexibility and choice. Companies will rethink the role of a single HQ in favor of a broader ecosystem of work sites that may include regional offices, coworking spaces, and home to support increasing and ongoing mobility.

3. ***Space allocations will favor "we space" over "me space."***
   To influence employees to use the office as their destination of choice, occupiers must rethink what their offices can deliver that is unique compared to the experience of working remote.

4. ***Conferencing will adapt to "mixed presence" collaboration.***
   Technology that connects on-site employees to remote employees will become standard builds in conference rooms. Tools such as virtual whiteboarding

software, smartboards, synchronous and asynchronous communication platforms and large format telepresence devices will lessen the disadvantages of virtually joining an in-person meeting.

5. **Amenities strategies will focus on hospitality and services.**

To create a "magnetized" office that people want to come to, amenities will focus on creating a welcoming environment, supporting employee health & well-being and enhancing the convenience of working on-site. The office's new purpose will be to provide a venue for community, culture and collaboration. Employees will be spending less time on individual/focused tasks while on-site and more time collaborating, networking and socializing. The composition of the office will adjust to reflect this change.

6. **Desk sharing occupancy strategies will continue to grow in popularity.**

"Free-address" occupancy strategies that entail desk sharing — with enhanced cleaning protocols to support health and safety — are an increasingly attractive solution for occupiers that wish to optimize office utilization in a more mobile future world.

7. **Employees will demand more "elbow room."**

The pandemic will have a lasting impact on employee consciousness of health and well-being in the workplace. Beyond requirements for physical distancing, workstations and conference rooms will continue to be reconfigured to allow for greater separation between employees. Occupiers will not necessarily need to buy new, larger furniture standards though. Most will address these concerns via neighborhood planning and circulation

8. **Healthy building design and operation will take center stage.**

COVID-19 has underscored the connection between buildings and wellness. As landlords and employees *compete for tenants and employees respectively, differentiated workplace environments will be those that innovate in the field of well-being in the workplace and address a broad spectrum of health beyond just the physical.*

9. **How we define and measure workplace performance will change.**
   If workplaces exist to support the business enterprise and the people who occupy them, CRE success metrics should present a balanced scorecard and align to broader company goals. People-centric measures will become more common in the future to reflect the holistic intentions of workplace design.

10. **Partnerships between CRE, HR and IT will strengthen.**
    More than ever before, delivering a high-performing workplace experience will depend on the thoughtful integration of space, people and technology. To navigate this interdisciplinary field, we will likely see an evolution in the role of "Head of Corporate Real Estate" towards a more elevated and strategic position of "Chief Places Officer."

Its interesting to note that all this has been covered thru the length and breadth if the book!

7.8 The Future Right Agenda: Green to Blue:

The Future belongs to the Millennials, who would form 75% of the Work force by 2025; according to Harvard Business Review Posting "Sustainability is set to become an even more important issue when Millennials (1981-2001), the biggest generation, have settled down."

Millennials are well informed and they value sustainable consumption. 66% say they are willing to pay more for services by brands, companies that are committed to creating a positive environmental impact.

So, the Employees of the Future are Changing and the offices need to respond to that! Traditional ways of brick-and-mortar building need to be ruled out in favour of more ideation-based re-use concepts of available spaces with the right inherent attributes.

The Future belongs to a new way of thinking out a Positive work space in making one that has a "Positive Impact" at a global level. It is famously known that "There is no Plan B and certainly no Planet B"; so environmental issues are slowly gaining speed in the way we make our new Work spaces as well as other types of built environment.

The cause of the Circular Design (Broadhurst, Miciunas, Nowak, Schipper, & Wheeler, 2021) is championed by the Ellen MacArthur Foundation, and is based on the principles of designing out waste and pollution, keeping products and materials in use, and regenerating natural systems.

Compared to a linear economy of "take-make-waste," a circular economy is based on "reduce-reuse-recover" strategies for materials in closed-loop systems. In a linear economy, resources are taken from the ground to make products which are used until no longer needed, at which point they are discarded — i.e., "thrown away." The circular economy, however, acknowledges that there is no place on our planet called "away" to responsibly dispose of these products. Thus, in a circular economy, products and services are designed with materials, that are upcycled or recycled, at the end of their useful life.

Accordingly, The New Agenda for Change, as suggested by a Caitlin Turner, Senior Principal, ID, HOK ((Turner, 2021) "To create a future-ready evolved workplace, commit to designing spaces that are not only environmentally sustainable, but that **go beyond green to become blue**. Green spaces traditionally focus on the environmental impact whereas blue spaces focus on the wellbeing of occupants in addition to the environment."

Accordingly, she mentions that a sustainable future depends on Core Blue Principles: Regenerative spaces; Carbon neutrality; Reducing Embodied Carbon; and Leveraging Circularity in Design.

"There is growing need to re-think this more than just thinking Green thru Landscape and horticulture, but to actually — rethink materials, consider patterns that emulate nature, select diffused lighting, and leverage outdoor workspaces with provisions for solar screening, power, and enhanced technology."

If you actually look at this shift from what's Called "Green to BLUE", the fact is this has been actually practiced for centuries and for this one has to look no further than the Japanese way of life: Wabi-Sabi which means beauty in that which is temporary or imperfect. In the Wabi-Sabi way of thinking, everything is temporary / unfinished (work in progress) and yet everything is perfect just the way it is!

Is this not the same, as what we are veering towards, when we mention a "Blue Approach" or "Circular Design" or "The 3R's: Reduce, Re-use & Re-cycle". Is Wabi-Sabi not a metaphor for the approach that is needed ahead! Can our work spaces be truly Positive by being environmentally responsible and nature positive!?

Is there any connection in Wabi-Sabi and Ikigai both being Japanese concepts that both relate to secrets of longevity and happiness? As per the Japanese best seller book on Ikigai (Garcia & Miralles, 2017), the authors interviewed the residents of the Japanese village with the highest percentage of 100-year-olds—one of the world's Blue Zones. *Ikigai* reveals the secrets to their longevity and happiness: how they eat, how they move, how they work, how they foster collaboration and community, and—their best-kept secret— how they find the *ikigai* that brings satisfaction to their lives. And it provides practical tools to help you discover your own *ikigai*. Because who doesn't want to find happiness in every day?

Maybe after all, it's a case of looking at a Positive Built environment by accepting the inherent beauty of our historical building and sites and looking at each opportunity to retain the old and refrain displacement and destruction of the older built environment.

What we would need to understand is that Imperfections do not affect a positive work space environment, in fact they make the spaces more authentic. The imperfections in the existing stock of built space in any city are actually the beauty and humanness of the place. I believe this is a step towards positivity as well.

Endnote

A Lot is said on whether the Work Place will survive? Is the Pandemic the end of the Work place?

Experts seem unanimous, and so do i: **The Work space will survive, and indeed Thrive**... but in a new form, as discussed in previous chapters.

The Much-Quoted paper (Wernick & Morris, 2020) claims that "the COVID-19 pandemic has been the largest remote working experiment in history and presents a transformational opportunity to reimagine the new workplace. Employees have changed and are expecting their workplaces to change as well. Leadership is taking action – less than one in five executives say they want to return to the office as it was pre-pandemic."

People will come to offices for reasons as best described by this article (Wernick & Morris, 2020), as the three key drivers :

*"The first driver, **Collaboration**, is an obvious one. That's not to say that all virtual collaboration is challenging, however certain types such as group brainstorming and ideating are difficult to do remotely. Whether it be sketching, pinning up, or strategic business planning – the virtual tools still cannot replace in-person interactions.*

*The second driver, **Serendipitous Encounters**, are non-existent in the work from home world. Occurrences like running into a colleague while grabbing coffee or quickly exchanging ideas while walking to a meeting simply cannot happen while working remotely. Cross-functional knowledge sharing is sorely lacking without communal spaces designed to facilitate it. According to research by Cushman & Wakefield, over a third of employees engaged in remote work during the pandemic do not feel like they are learning. Specifically, formal process learning is continuing but informal learning and mentoring are challenged.*[2]

*The last driver to the office is **Connection to Community and Culture**. Over our 30 years of designing workplaces, we've found that this is what distinguishes incredible organizations. Workers want to be connected to their colleagues, company mission and purpose. These are leading reasons for increased productivity, innovation and commitment. According to research, half of employees struggled to connect with their company's culture during the COVID-19-induced remote work experiment. Community doesn't only contribute to workers wellbeing, but also leads to better business outcomes. A successful workplace design will enhance a company's unique community and culture to massively inspire and engage their workforce."*

There is no doubt we are on the threshold of a God given opportunity for Change! Accordingly, The New Agenda for Change, as suggested by a Caitlin Turner, Senior Principal, ID, HOK (Turner, 2021)

"...COVID has handed us the opportunity to address what wasn't working..."

There is now the renewed need to create a newer and healthier future, one that addresses the core issues, as mentioned by Caitlin very clearly, that existed in pre pandemic times:

"... As people question whether the office is a thing of the past, we in turn must consider what the office of the future could look like. To do that, we must first acknowledge the flaws and gaps that existed in the workplace prior to the pandemic. Work-related stress and burnout were at an all-time high. Density of space was at capacity. Daily commuting was polluting the planet and draining our energy. Authenticity and meaningful human connection were missing, despite our ability to be more connected, than ever before."

In order to devise a new, healthier and more rewarding workspace, Turner rightly suggests that we must reconcile the core issues that shaped the pre-pandemic office:

- **Stress and burnout:** *undermined work-life balance, leaving the workforce largely disengaged. We need to empower the health and wellbeing of our largest asset — our people.*
- **Under-utilized, inflexible office space:** *We need to define the purpose of place and enable rapid, responsive change.*
- **Social inequity:** *was infrequently addressed. We need to create diverse, inclusive, welcoming, and humane spaces for all.*
- **Social connection:** *was tenuous and shallow. We need to help people reconnect authentically, to help them feel*

safe and valued, and to empower them with options, choice and control.

- **Rapid evolution of technology:** was having significant impacts, both positive and negative, on spaces and people. We need to ensure balance.
- **Focus on productivity:** was myopic. We need to shift our focus to innovation, to ensure business continuity and relevance.
- **Hygiene and cleanliness practices:** were stagnant. We need new, enhanced ways to address cleanliness and durability, and must look for opportunities to reduce touchpoints.
- **Talent retention and upskilling:** were often an afterthought. We need to embed lifelong learning opportunities, enable mentorship and knowledge transfer, and rethink when, where and how we work to keep our workforce relevant and engaged.
- **Climate change action:** has been passively addressed. We need to go beyond simply meeting certification and tackle time-sensitive environmental issues in a holistic, comprehensive manner.

We must imagine physical spaces and best practices that truly address our needs, both now and in the future."

This book hopes to have addressed these matters.

My Take: The Future Work spaces shall find Positivity in new ways and would be a combination of these 10 Aspects depending on Context & Culture:

I. **Decentralized (Neighbourhood based)**
II. **Non-Ownership based (Increased sharing of resources)**
III. **Culture connected (The Eternal Glue)**
IV. **Social (Collaborative Clubs)**
V. **Biophilic (Nature related)**
VI. **Balanced ME / WE based (Human needs based)**
VII. **Hygiene Focussed (Touchless & contactless)**
VIII. **Technology Enabled (Virtual meets Physical)**
IX. **Blue in addition to Green (Sustainable + Circular)**
X. **Disruption Ready (Bring it on!)**

They say: A Good Architect Always has Plans! And we must build our plans around the above 10 predictions for a positive work space.

MY PLANS, thru this BOOK, were to stir up the Pot and stoke the fires to debate what promotes positivity at the work place! The 925 Zombie Story was the only story in the book, the rest are facts gleaned out of research and squeezed out of experience.

This book is meant to be a friend and a reference point for practitioners and people dealing with the work space. It would not be, if it only told stories.

This book was never meant for one kind of reader or one kind of patron! It has been deliberately cross disciplinary and embracing of all perspectives; of course, there could be some who disagree with the basic notion of reversing the Maslow's Pyramid, but this is the premise of this book! You may agree or you may disagree.

To different people, this book will have meant different things and would lead to different perspectives and take-aways. That's the idea: Work space Positivity is Not one dimensional and needs a multi-dimensional approach to viewing things!

Everyone would identify with the problems of the contemporary work place, as delved into Chapter 1, with some problems being more relatable and others less, depending on which city and country you come from! That's fine and that helps develop a Global perspective on things!

If you are a Behavioural Psychologist or a Human resources person, you would relate to Chapter 2, 3 and 4, though they do turn Maslow's Hierarchy of Needs on its head in a Post Pandemic Scenario. You may agree or you may agree to disagree; this is my view point on how the times have changed and how we need to understand that the very physicality / physiology of the work place needs to be re-questioned and re-imagined.

If you are a Student of Design, a young architect at a work places: you will feel enthused by the fact that Design can and would continue to play a key role in shaping "positivity" in the work place! For you Chapters 5 & 6 must be read again and again and applies if not fully, atleast in parts to your way of thinking and some day: in your ways of working!

If you are a seasoned work space manager or an experienced "seen it all" architect, you may agree that "Context is everything" and the applicability of different principles depends on different contextual reference points. The differing reference points may relate to different contexts, geographies, economies, service verticals, organisational types and finally people types!

But what you all would agree as well is that "Culture at the work place is everything" and that much of it can be shaped with a work place design that works better!

If you are a Facility Manager or project manager, you would agree with Chapter 7 that Talks of getting it Right and would perhaps have more to add on with your years of experience and enterprise. That's what this book tries to do …. It gives you blank pages at the end to scribble your thoughts and your take away, where you agree and where you disagree. In doing so, it makes you take a stand and in making you do so, is the success of this book: reduced fence sitters and more people taking a stand, on what it means to them to create positivity at the work place, where we spend our most meaningful waking hours.

And Most Importantly, if you are a client, this book would have given you a sense of "WHY" Architects are needed, even more in Post pandemic Times, to design work spaces that are meaningful, engaging & productive! It would establish the multiple level of thoughts and engagement an architect needs to put into creating a work space that works! Good Design, I say again, is Not Google searching: It is Soul searching! Its about understanding the most complex thing on earth: The end user: The Human being!

The happiness of this end user: as a human being is the most important aspect of design! Remember what Sir Richard Branson, founder of Virgin Group said: "If you look after your staff, they'll look after your customers. It's that simple".

The Bottom line is: Do what you can, in whichever area of influence you can, to create a Positive Work place, that is good for all. Its Good for the Business!

A Positive Work place = Positive Business Place

Acknowledgements

This has been a Book born in Pandemic Times, with no access to libraries or erstwhile ways of research that I was used to when I did my Thesis 30 years back from the School of Planning & Architecture, New Delhi, that won the best Thesis of the batch. That was then, but it starts from thanking and recognising the teachers and mentors who helped shape and mould my mind.

No acknowledgement would start without remembering and respecting my Late Maverick professor Anil Laul, who was a God for most of us and the beacon of light we all had to follow; following him and his journey to writing his own Book, a few years before he left us, was the start of the inspiration for this book.

Thanks to my wonderful family and two children Rayan and Myrrene, who know when to leave me in my Zone / Flow, as mentioned in this book, to write this book in quick time period of 60 days. And the fullest of thanks to my wife Arnaz, who has been supportive, silent and stoic in support, at our Studio and at home, in managing thru the few ups and more downs, post the pandemic!

Finally, my friends, batchmates, my studio and parents...all of whom have supported and encouraged me in this journey for my first book, that certainly will not be my last!

A Special Line of thanks to the sponsors of this Book: HNI India and their spontaneous support extended for a worthy cause, such as this book!

Support Tashana

The Proceeds of this Book would encourage part percentage donation to a Trust Founded by my dear wife Arnaz called TASHANA (The Abode of Hope to Support & Nurture Animals) that has been focussed on feeding and taking care of stray dogs that live on the streets and whom no one loves or care for, mostly!

The Idea was to start when the lock down was imposed and we started feeding 20-30 dogs daily till we narrowed down on 6 dogs of a litter that we practically raised from puppies to full grown dogs 12 months old today! One of them sits in our home and 5 others still get fed by us every day in the evening including other dogs around. The trust also inculcates love for animals, by developing and supporting children, who play on the street, to spend half an hour at least daily in becoming more dog loving and friendly! The Trust intends to support these children in their education and basic needs as it grows.

The Tashana trust aims to grow to other spaces and areas, where dogs can be reared in their own back yards in familiar surroundings with children from their own neighbourhoods. A small start, but one with its heart in the right place.

Do write in to Tashana at arnazv@gmail.com

About The Author

The Author Vistasp Bhagwagar is an Architect with 30 years of Work experience having graduated from the School of Planning and Architecture, New Delhi, in 2021, with two Gold medals and lots of passion towards the field of design. He went to UK on a full British Chevening Scholarship in 1993-94 to do an MA Course in Urban Design, from Oxford Brookes University, UK.

After returning to India, he started Architect Vistasp & Associates (A Design Consulting Firm) that focussed on Commercial Work space and Public Space design for the next 25 years. Today AVA Design Pvt Ltd, as it's known, is a 35-person Boutique design firm that works in the areas of workspace design, retail, commercial, institutional, hospitality and related architecture and is the recipients of several awards, accolades and featured publications. It also works in collaboration with other associates in Bangalore, Ahmedabad, Hyderabad and Mumbai.

He is also the Co-Founder and mentor of the Story Boxx initiative (www.thestoryboxx.com) that connects materials to architects thru a technology platform, enabling better samples outreach to the design community at large in India.

Apart from being an architect, friends know Vistasp as being an avid cartoonist and poet at heart with over 80 poems to date: next book coming! Vistasp is a Thought Leader and Visionary who believes: One life: make it a Story Worth telling! This book is the first step to telling that story.

Your Thoughts

Bibliography

Aggarwal, P. (2018, Aug 29). *How To Create A Positive Workplace Culture*. Retrieved from Forbes: https://www.forbes.com/sites/pragyaagarwaleurope/2018/08/29/how-to-create-a-positive-work-place-culture/?sh=3df53ad24272

Architectural Concepts: Circulation. (2020). Retrieved from Portico.space: http://portico.space/journal//architectural-concepts-circulation

Awfis Editorial. (2018, September 21). Retrieved from awfis: https://www.awfis.com/inspiration/agile-versus-activity-based-working-which-one-will-you-choose

Beheshti, N. (2019, January 16). *10 Timely Statistics About The Connection Between Employee Engagement And Wellness*. Retrieved from Forbes: https://www.forbes.com/sites/nazbeheshti/2019/01/16/10-timely-statistics-about-the-connection-between-employee-engagement-and-wellness/?sh=6fafb48722a0

Ben Waber, J. M. (2014, October 1). *Workspaces That Move People*. Retrieved from Harvard Business Review: https://hbr.org/2014/10/workspaces-that-move-people

Boag, P. (2017, June 13). *Convincing Clients: How To Get Sign Off When It Matters*. Retrieved from Smashing Magazine: https://www.smashingmagazine.com/2017/06/convincing-clients-sign-off/

Broadhurst, N., Miciunas, g., Nowak, M., Schipper, D., & Wheeler, C. (2021, March). *An Interactive Tool For A Circular Economy In The Built Environment*. Retrieved from Work Design Magazine: https://www.workdesign.com/2021/03/an-interactive-tool-for-a-circular-economy-in-the-built-environment/?utm_source=Subscribers&utm_campaign=29f687e519-ManagingChange_EMAIL_CAMPAIGN_11__23_20_COPY_01&utm_medium=email&utm_term=0_add981fc0f-29f687e519-319817

Bureau, P. I. (2021, March 4). *(Release ID: 1702417) Visitor Counter : 8473.* Delhi: PIB. Retrieved from https://pib.gov.in/PressReleasePage.aspx?PRID=1702417

Carter, B. (2020, Jan 31). *12 Tips to Optimize your office space planning.* Retrieved from squarefoot.com: https://www.squarefoot.com/leasopedia/office-space-layout-planning-tips/

Cherry, K. (2021, January 13). *HAPPINESS.* Retrieved from Very Well Mind: https://www.verywellmind.com/what-is-flow-2794768

Cherry, K. (2021, March 15). *Self-Determination Theory and Motivation.* Retrieved from Very Well Mind: https://www.verywellmind.com/what-is-self-determination-theory-2795387

Cooper, S. (2012, July 30). *Forbes.* Retrieved from Make More Money By Making Your Employees Happy: https://www.forbes.com/sites/stevecooper/2012/07/30/make-more-money-by-making-your-employees-happy/?sh=6257ccdc5266

Council, F. A. (2017, January 9). *10 Characteristics To Look For In Your Next Client.* Retrieved from Forbes: https://www.forbes.com/sites/forbesagencycouncil/2017/01/09/10-

characteristics-agency-executives-look-for-in-clients/?sh= 1cf1a1b5712c

Decoraid. (2019). *EVERYTHING YOU NEED TO KNOW: 20 INTERIOR DESIGN STYLES DEFINED IN 2019*. Retrieved from Decoraid: https://www.decoraid.com/blog/ interior-design-styles-definition-2019

Definition of 'Ease Of Doing Business'. (2021). *The Economic Times E Paper*, 1. Retrieved from https://economictimes. indiatimes.com/definition/ease-of-doing-business

Ease of Doing Business Index. (n.d.). Retrieved from Wikipedia: https://en.wikipedia.org/wiki/Ease_of_doing_business_index

Friedman, R. (2014, August 4). *Schedule a 15-Minute Break Before You Burn Out*. Retrieved from Harvard Business Review: https://hbr.org/2014/08/schedule-a-15-minute- break-before-you-burn-out

Garcia, H., & Miralles, F. (2017). *Ikigai: The Japanese Secret to a Long and Happy Life.* Penguin.

Gierland, J. (1996, January 9). *Go With The Flow*. Retrieved from Wired: https://www.wired.com/1996/09/czik/

Great Place To Work Model. (n.d.). Retrieved from Great Place To Work: https://www.greatplacetowork.in/gptw-model/

GRIHA Rating. (n.d.). Retrieved from Green Rating for Integrated Habitat Assessment: https://www.grihaindia.org/griha-rating

hamill, L. (2019, February 4). *What An Inclusive Workplace Actually Looks Like, And Seven Ways To Achieve It*. Retrieved from Forbes: https://www.forbes.com/sites/ forbeshumanresourcescouncil/2019/02/04/what-an-inclusive-workplace-actually-looks-like-and-seven-ways-to-achieve-it/?sh=604ea36b316b

Institute, G. W. (2016, April 19). *What's the Difference Between Wellness and Well-being? Or is There One?* Retrieved from Global Wellness Institute: https://globalwellnessinstitute. org/global-wellness-institute-blog/2016/04/19/2016-4-19-whats-the-difference-between-wellness-and-well-being-or-is-there-one/

Jantsch, J. (unknown). *Understanding, Narrowing, and Choosing Your Ideal Client.* Retrieved from Duct tape Marketting: https://ducttapemarketing.com/choosing-ideal-client/

Jeffrey, k., Mahoney, S., Michaelson, J., & Abdallah, S. (2021). *Well-being at work.* Retrieved from NEf Consulting UK: https://www. nefconsulting.com/our-services/strategy-culture-change/wellbeing/wellbeing-at-work/

MacKay, J. (2020, January 29). *How to deal with burnout: Signs, symptoms, and strategies for getting you back on track after burning out.* Retrieved from Rescue Time Blog: https://rescuetime.wpengine.com/burnout-syndrome-recovery/#Types-of-burnout

Maloney, R. (2017, October 30). *Human-centric office lighting 'boosts productivity'.* Retrieved from Lux review: https://www. luxreview.com/2017/10/30/human-centric-office-lighting-boosts-productivity/#:~:text=Additionally%2C%20the%20 participants%20working%20in,and%2050%20per%20 cent%20healthier.

Miller, K. (2020, March 19). *5 CRITICAL STEPS IN THE CHANGE MANAGEMENT PROCESS.* Retrieved from Harvard Business Schoool Online: https://online.hbs.edu/blog/post/change-management-process

Miscowich, P., & Puybaraud, M. (2021). *Shaping Today's Workplace For The "High-Performing" Workplace Of Tomorrow.* Retrieved from WORK DESIGN: https://www.workdesign.com/2021/02/shaping-todays-workplace-for-the-high-performing-workplace-of-tomorrow/

Netrix. (2019, November 22). *The Top 3 AV Trends in the Workplace for 2020.* Retrieved from Netrix: https://netrixllc.com/blog/top-workplace-av-trends-2020/

Philips. (2015). *Philips Lighting Industry research Summary.* Retrieved from phlips: http://www.newscenter.philips.com/main/standard/resources/lighting/press/2015/Office-Lighting/Philips-Lighting-industry-research-summary.pdf

PREMACK, R. (2018, August 2). *17 seriously disturbing facts about your job.* Retrieved from Business Insider India: https://www.businessinsider.in/17-seriously-disturbing-facts-about-your-job/articleshow/65246844.cms

Putnam, L. (2015). Workplace Wellness That Works. In L. Putnam, *10 Steps to Infuse Well being and Vitality into any organization* (p. 315). New jersey: Wiley India Pvt Ltd.

release, N. (2021, january 21). *Better than normal? Living, working, playing and leading in 2021.* Retrieved from JLL: https://www.us.jll.com/en/newsroom/jll-reports-better-than-normal-vision-2021

Ryan, P. (2021). *Working.* Retrieved from JLL: https://images.hello.jll.com/Web/JLLAmericas/%7Bc380d754-697d-434a-9223-d021d748eace%7D_VISION-2021-WORKING-BETTER-OFFICE-20200121.pdf

Seiter, C. (2014, August 21). *The Science of Taking Breaks at Work: How to Be More Productive By Changing the Way You*

Think About Downtime. Retrieved from Buffer: https://buffer.com/resources/science-taking-breaks-at-work/

Seppala, E., & Cameron, K. (2015, December 1). *Proof That Positive Work Cultures Are More Productive*. Retrieved from harvard Business Review: https://hbr.org/2015/12/proof-that-positive-work-cultures-are-more-productive

Sharma, N. (2021, March 5). *Bengaluru, Shimla ranked 'most livable' cities in government's Ease of Living Index 2020*. Retrieved from The Economic Times: https://m.economictimes.com/news/economy/indicators/bengaluru-shimla-ranked-most-livable-cities-in-govts-ease-of-living-index-2020/amp_articleshow/81327639.cms

Sharpe, N. (2019, February 27). *Coffee: A Workplace Saviour or productivity Killer*. Retrieved from Organized Assistant: https://organizedassistant.com/coffee-productivity/

Sharpe, N. (2019, Feb 27). *Coffee: A Workplace Saviour Or Productivity Killer?* Retrieved from Organisedassistant: https://organizedassistant.com/coffee-productivity/

Smith, R. (n.d.). *Art In The Workplace: Why You Need It And How To Choose It*. Retrieved from Work design: https://www.workdesign.com/2016/10/art-workplace-need-choose/

Taylor, C. (2019, July 11). *Workers value a strong company culture over higher pay, study claims*. Retrieved from CNBC: https://www.cnbc.com/2019/07/11/workers-value-a-strong-company-culture-over-higher-pay-study-claims.html

Thamjarat, T. (2017, February 17). *What makes people most happy?* Retrieved from Medium: https://medium.com/@V_TNO/what-makes-people-most-happy-60578716fb92

The 10 Most Common Problems People Have at Work and How to Solve Them. (n.d.). Retrieved from The International Psychology Clinic: https://theinternationalpsychologyclinic. com/the-10-most-common-problems-people-have-at-work-and-how-to-solve-them/

Turner, C. (2021). *Emerging Into A New Ecosystem Of Work.* Retrieved from Work Design Magazine: https:// www.workdesign.com/2021/03/emerging-into-a-new-ecosystem-of-work/?utm_source=Subscribers&utm_ campaign=ee8e5dc753-ManagingChange_EMAIL_ CAMPAIGN_11__23_20_COPY_01&utm_medium=email&utm_ term=0_add981fc0f-ee8e5dc753-319817021

Unknown. (2018, July 6). *Key Concepts & Shared Language.* Retrieved from Nirsa: https://nirsa.net/nirsa/portfolio-items/ health-and-wellbeing-key-concepts/

Unknown. (2018, July 16). *Wellness vs. Wellbeing Programs: What's the difference?* Retrieved from Triton HR: https://www.tritonhr.com/blog/ wellness-vs-wellbeing-programs-whats-the-difference/

unknown. (2020, April). *COVID-19:.* Retrieved from Ginger.IO: https://assets.website-files. com/5cbad46537d84e6404551ac1/5e8e6c50da07f0a5df14d ba6_Workplace_Attitudes_2020_Preview_R4.pdf

unknown. (2020, Q4 unknown). *Well Building Standard.* Retrieved from Well Certified: https://standard.wellcertified.com/well

unknown. (2021, jan 4). *Hot AV Trends 2021 to Watch Out For and Adapt to What Lies Ahead.* Retrieved from actis: https:// www.actis.co.in/av-trends-2021-to-watch-out-for

unknown. (n.d.). *7 Must-Have Tech Tools for the Modern Office.* Retrieved from theresepctionist: https://thereceptionist.com/blog/7-must-have-tech-tools-for-the-modern-office/

Unknown. (n.d.). *Ease of Doing Business.* Retrieved from Make in India: https://www.makeinindia.com/eodb

Unknown. (n.d.). *Emotional Intelligence.* Retrieved from Corporate Finance Institute: https://corporatefinanceinstitute.com/resources/careers/soft-skills/emotional-intelligence-quotient-eq/

unknown. (Unknown). *HOW TO SYSTEMATICALLY CHOOSE THE RIGHT CONTRACTOR.* Retrieved from Sebring Design Build: https://sebringdesignbuild.com/how-to-systematically-choose-the-right-contractor/

Vallina, A. S., Alegre, J., & Guerrero, R. F. (2018). Happiness at work in knowledge-intensive contexts: Opening the research agenda. *European Research on Management and Business Economics*, 149-159. Retrieved from science direct: https://www.sciencedirect.com/science/article/pii/S2444883418300883#bib0485

Vanderland, B. B. (n.d.). *Is Your office Designed for Inclusion.* Retrieved from Work Design: https://www.workdesign.com/2016/09/office-designed-inclusion/

Vierling, L. (2021, January). *The Hybrid Post-Pandemic Workplace: Preparing The Workforce For Change.* Retrieved from Work Design Magazine: https://www.workdesign.com/2021/01/the-hybrid-post-pandemic-workplace-preparing-the-workforce-for-change/

Vrabie, A. (2013, October 18). *Stefan Sagmeister interview - The Happy Show artist on work and happiness.* Retrieved from Sandglaz Blog: https://blog.sandglaz.com/stefan-sagmeister-interview-happy-show/

Watt, M. (2019, April 11). *Understanding LEED, WELL, and the Differences*. Retrieved from Environmental Protection: https://eponline.com/Articles/2019/04/11/Understanding-LEED-WELL-and-the-Differences.aspx?Page=1

website. (2021). *AI-powered solutions for enterprises to become hybrid workplaces*. Retrieved from smartenspaces: https://smartenspaces.com/solutions/hybrid-workplace?gclid=EAIaIQobChMIm-bAhJGJ7wIVsTdyCh0yGgEuEAAYASAAEgK4q_D_BwE

Website, C. (n.d.). *Cost-effective ways to control office acoustics*. Retrieved from Sound Zero: https://sound-zero.com/cost-effective-ways-to-control-office-acoustics/

Weckerling, E. (n.d.). *10 Tips For Creating A Sustainable Office*. Retrieved from Work Design: https://www.workdesign.com/2019/04/10-tips-for-creating-a-sustainable-office/

Whalen, C. (2020, january 20). *The Benefits of a Positive Work Environment*. Retrieved from Office Partners on Pearl: https://officepartnersonpearl.com/the-benefits-of-a-positive-work-environment/#:~:text=Research%20shows%20that%20a%20happy,12%25%20spike%20in%20employee%20productivity.&text=A%20positive%20environment%20breeds%20employees,motivated%2C%20and%20work%20more%

What is the PERMA Model? . (n.d.). Retrieved from Corporate Finance Institute: https://corporatefinanceinstitute.com/resources/careers/soft-skills/perma-model/

White, D. P. (2017, Feb 19). *The Vibrant Workplace*. Retrieved from connectionculture.com: https://www.connectionculture.com/post/the-vibrant-workplace

WILHELMSEN, T. R. (2019, April 23). *15 Practice Areas Critical to Achieving a Great Workplace*. Retrieved from Great Place To Work: https://www.greatplacetowork.com/resources/blog/15-practice-areas-critical-to-achieving-a-great-workplace

Wilkins, B. (n.d.). *Stimulating Biophilia Through Corporate Interior Design*. Retrieved from workdesign: https://www.workdesign.com/2021/02/stimulating-biophilia-through-corporate-interior-design/

Wilson, G. (n.d.). *Maslow's Theory of Motivation: Driving Your Teams to Success*. Retrieved from Success factory: https://www.thesuccessfactory.co.uk/blog/maslows-theory-of-motivation-driving-your-teams-to-success#:~:text=Maslow's%20hierarchy%20of%20needs%20is,Human%20Motivation%22%20in%20Psychological%20Review.&text=He%20stated%20that%20the%20needs,to%20needs%20high

HNI Corporation is a leading provider of workplace furnishings and residential building products. Their recognized family of global brands, namely Allsteel, HBF, HON, Gunlocke, HNI Lamex and HNI India are among the strongest, most widely known and respected in the industry.

Each brand in their portfolio brings along a unique character to their offering including different styles, stories, and solutions. Allsteel for example is a workplace research driven brand, that specializes in providing modular office furniture solutions. Gunlocke on the other hand, with its unparalleled human craftmanship, has a history so rich it has even furnished the Oval Office and had eight US Presidents seated in the iconic Washington Chair. HBF is a brand that works with luminaries of the industry, making wood veneer and lounge products that are timeless, yet contemporary in design. HNI Lamex and HNI India are contract-driven leader brands in Asia known for customized office solutions.

HNI Corporation has been on the Forbes list of America's Most Trustworthy Companies and has been recognized by Newsweek Magazine for America's Most Responsible Companies in 2020 & 2021. They use sustainable practices to create products that are designed for the environment, manufactured responsibly, and delivered efficiently. From 2020, with an intent to create sustainable environments for all stakeholders they have become signatory to UN Global Compact, dedicating themselves to the core principles of human rights, labor fairness, environmental protection and anti-corruption, while also aligning their business with the Sustainable Development Goals

The capability of their manufacturing and the strength of their distribution enables them to provide the best workplace furnishings solutions to meet the needs of every customer. HNI designs solutions for all spaces in an office, which include workstations, seating solutions, collaborative solutions, and wide range of private office and conference room solutions.

CPSIA information can be obtained
at www.ICGtesting.com
Printed in the USA
BVHW052023060921
616156BV00002B/119

9 781543 707793